Wheel-Thrown
Pottery

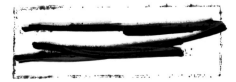

Wheel-Thrown
Pottery

Bill van Gilder
and Cara Biasucci

LARK BOOKS

A Division of Sterling Publishing Co., Inc.
New York

Series Editor:	Dawn Cusick
Series Designer:	Thom Gaines
Art Production:	Jackie Kerr, Matt Paden
Cover Designer:	DIY Network, Stewart Pack
Assistant Editor:	Matt Paden
Contributing Writer:	Jane Laferla
Photographer:	C. Kurt Holter
Photography Director:	Chris Bryant

10 9 8 7 6 5 4 3 2 1

First Edition

Published by Lark Books, A Division of
Sterling Publishing Co., Inc.
387 Park Avenue South, New York, N.Y. 10016

738.1
VAN

Distributed in Canada by Sterling Publishing,
c/o Canadian Manda Group, 165 Dufferin Street
Toronto, Ontario, Canada M6K 3H6

Distributed in the United Kingdom by GMC Distribution Services,
Castle Place, 166 High Street, Lewes, East Sussex, England BN7 1XU

Distributed in Australia by Capricorn Link (Australia) Pty Ltd.,
P.O. Box 704, Windsor, NSW 2756 Australia

If you have questions or comments about this book, please contact:
Lark Books
67 Broadway
Asheville, NC 28801
(828) 253-0467

Manufactured in China

ISBN 13: 978-1-57990-855-3
ISBN 10: 1-57990-855-1

For information about custom editions, special sales, premium and corporate purchases, please contact Sterling Special Sales Department at 800-805-5489 or specialsales@sterlingpub.com.

Contents

Wheel-Thrown Pottery

As you grab that first lump of clay, know that it's going to grab you. When I was 15 years old, a teacher put a piece of clay into my hands and showed me a movie about wheel throwing. I was hooked. By following the process, I experienced the satisfaction and joy that comes from making something by connecting my creative mind to my eyes and hands. And you will, too. That's the magic of working with clay.

I've been making pots for almost 40 years now, and still find it incredibly exciting to go to the studio every day. As much as I teach clay to others, I've learned that clay teaches me constantly. Working with clay is a partnership — you get as much out of it as you give. Making pottery is not something anyone can give you. It takes practice and is user friendly as long as you know what you want to do.

On my DIY Network show *Throwing Clay* I present a common-sense approach to working with clay, and I've tried to mirror that approach in this book. We all have to learn the basics, but it's just as essential to learn to respect each step in the process — from kneading the clay to opening the loaded kiln. Envisioning what you're making in your mind's eye from the very beginning brings success. The clay on the wheel is only one step. If you haven't prepared the clay properly for that moment, all else will be for naught.

This book is set up to take you from the basics, including learning about tools and techniques to making advanced projects. The book gives enough technical information on throwing, trimming, waxing, and glazing to complete 11 functional projects with 11 tried-and-true glaze recipes. Each project allows you to build skills while learning about form, scale, and finish in relation to function. For more advanced potters, every project leaves ample room for innovation, giving you the opportunity to take them to places I might never have considered.
In the past, potters filled a need in their societies by providing the vessels used for everday life. Today, potters fulfill a need of another sort, which is more the soulful or spiritual side of making things by hand. The more we sit behind our computers, the more we need that handmade mug, serving bowl, or plate in our lives to ground us. They not only connect us to earth materials, they connect us by touch to all the thought, emotion, and creativity that went into making them.

I believe the quiet pot speaks the loudest. If I had to choose one ceramic piece that I consider the highest form of the craft, it would be a Korean covered jar made during the Yi Dynasty. Thrown by a nameless potter, and probably one of many made in huge quantities, everything fits the form in the right proportion, the lid in relationship to the foot, the faceting, the glazed surface — all meld perfectly. Aside from its technical perfection, the jar also has a wonderful sense of spontaneity about it that communicates, through the centuries, the joy of working in clay.

Teaching through my show on DIY Network has enabled me to hear from students across the country. I find I learn just as much from the hundreds of e-mails they send me as I hope they learn from me. I've come to understand that every potter — whether new to the craft or with years of experience — is a link in the long history of ceramics, and as each of us strives to do the best work we can, the chain only gets stronger. So I encourage you to read this book, find a potter to watch, and have fun. Most of all, as you hold that finished pot in your hands for the first time, celebrate your success!

Bill van Gilder,
Host of DIY Network's *Throwing Clay*

1

Wheel-Throwing Basics

Every potter knows the moment. Was it the beauty you saw in a particular vessel? Was it an inner urge to touch the earth in a creative way? Whatever your inspiration for wanting to learn to throw clay—welcome! This chapter will lead you through the basics, covering the tools, materials, and techniques you need to get started. You'll find discussions about choosing a kiln and clay, as well as instructions for kneading, centering, and opening a form. As in learning any skill, throwing clay takes practice and persistence. I encourage you to take time to master these basic techniques. Once you do, you'll be well on your way to to exploring new forms and an infinite range of design possibilities.

TOOLS & MATERIALS

Finding pottery tools and materials is surprisingly easy. If you don't have a pottery center in your town, getting what you need is as close as the internet, or a phone call away. My advice is to stick with the basics when starting out. You don't need every piece of equipment or tool available. To make it easier for you, the photo on page 14 shows all the tools you'll need for making the projects. The information in this section will also help you when setting up your own studio or when needing to understand what to look for when sharing a space.

POTTERY WHEELS

Wheels all serve the same function: they rotate the clay within a range of uniform speed, allowing you to shape the form you're throwing. If you're just starting to put together your own studio, you may be familiar with wheels you have used in classes or when using another potter's equipment. You may already have a feel for your comfort zone and know the features you may want for your own wheel.

If you don't know where to begin, talk to other potter's for advice and recommendations. Familiarize yourself with the variety of wheels available by reading the ads in various ceramics' magazines or doing a web search. The ads or sites will give you contact information for the manufacturer who will gladly answer any of your questions.

Choosing the right kiln depends on several factors—the size pottery you intend to make, the amount of space you have in your studio, and the type of electric power available to you. Kilns range in size from small, top-loading models that plug into a dryer outlet, to medium-sized kilns needing an electric receptacle similar to one used for a kitchen stove, and larger models with front-opening doors that can accommodate sculpture.

You will use your kiln both for the lower-temperature bisque firing that hardens the clay to receive glaze, and for your final high-firing. Since high-firing requires that the kiln reach average temperatures of between 1880 and 2250° Fahrenheit, electric kilns have heating elements that can withstand high temperatures, as well as linings made of insulating fire brick. Every kiln should have a kiln stand that creates an insulating layer of air between the bottom of the kiln and the studio floor. A kiln should also have a venting system.

Kilns have an external control panel that allow you to control the firing, and most panels are now computerized. Electric kilns have peephole plugs so you can see inside. Anytime you look inside a kiln, you must wear special safety glasses.

CONES

In addition to using the kiln controls to monitor temperatures when firing, potters use cones inside the kiln to help them determine what is known as the heat work, or exactly how much heat is going into the ceramic. Cones are made of the materials being fired and melt consistently at the same temperature each time. Cones are rigid when you put them in the kiln, and melt into a curved claw-like shape when they reach the proper temperature

Cones have assigned numbers, known as cone levels, that denote their rate of melting. For example, cones 07 and 08 would be used for bisque firing while cone 06 would be used for firing glazes. In other words, the higher the cone number, the hotter the kiln temperature.

CLAY

There are many clays available to potters—from low-fire to mid-range earthen ware to high-fired stoneware and porcelains. Clays also range in color from white to black. How do you choose? When making functional pottery, use a smooth, fine, clay body, since they're more durable in the long run than using coarse clay. Their tighter mass means they'll chip less and will withstand use in the microwave or repeated cycles in the dishwasher. If you want a bright glaze, select a light-toned clay (gray or white). If you want a glaze with depth and richness, start with a dark-toned clay (tan, red, brown, or black).

Because clay shrinks when it's dried and fired, you will want to know the shrinkage percentage rate of the clay you use. This is particularly necessary if you're making a piece that has a specific capacity, like a quart casserole, or a 12-ounce mug. For example, a mug made to hold 12 ounces of liquid will have to be made at the wet stage as a 14-ounce container, allowing for shrinkage to 12 ounces. You also want to make sure the clay is the right consistency for your project. You want to use softer clay for flat and small forms, and a stiffer clay for tall and large forms.

GLAZES

Glazes are all about the chemical interaction between clay, silica, and metal oxides when they meet fire. But don't let the chemistry frighten you. If you're inclined toward scientific thought, you'll be able to find extensive articles about glazes and the intricacies of their chemical processes. If you're more about the art, knowing a few basic principles is all you need.

Glaze Recipes. Silica, the prime ingredient of glaze, is mixed with water and other minerals before being applied to a clay form. By firing the form in the kiln, the silica and minerals melt to glass to create the smooth surface we all identify with glazed pottery. Adding metal oxides into the mix before it's applied to the clay form results in colored surfaces. The glazes look nothing like the final color when applied—it takes the heat of the kiln to transform the silica, minerals, and oxides to the intended color.

Glaze recipes ensure you can reproduce glaze colors. Each project in the book will have it's own glaze recipe or recipes. You'll also learn how to make glaze test tiles that will help you keep track of your recipes.

Safety Concerns. If you're glazing functional pottery to be used with food and drink, be sure the glazes are chemically balanced for food safety. All the glaze recipes used in this book are food-, microwave-, dishwasher-, and oven-safe. They have durable surfaces, and are calculated to fit the average clay body.

Always use the appropriate safety precautions when handling glaze-making materials. These include working in a well-ventilated room, wearing a respirator, and, when necessary, wearing rubber gloves.

TOOLS AROUND THE HOUSE

Wake up to the potential! Some of the best pottery tools are actually hiding in your kitchen drawer. While it may be handy to think of grabbing a kitchen tool to use in the studio, think twice before washing it and slipping it back. You don't want to use tools for food preparation if they've been mucking in the clay all day—buy duplicates strictly for studio use. Here's a list of household tools and their uses for making pottery. However, if you set your imagination to it, the list can be practically endless.

- A wired cheese slicer for cutting and faceting soft pots

- A pasta crimping tool for creating linear textures

- A cheese grater for making roughened surfaces, and at the same time putting shapes other than round into your forms

- Whisks for stirring and breaking up settled glazes

- Butter paddles for making corrugated textures

TOOLS

You can purchase tools, you can make your own customized tools, and some tools you can even find around the house. However, having the right tool near at hand is essential for your success when throwing clay. Many of the tools you'll need to make all the projects in this book are shown in the photo below. It's wise to put together a toolbox to keep your tools organized, accessible, and portable. An oversize tackle box is great for this purpose.

Tools have not changed very much throughout the whole history of pottery, though the materials they're made from has changed; some are now plastic or made from different types of rubber. When you go shopping for tools, you'll find that for every tool there are several versions available. Look for tools that fit your style of work. You'll eventually discover that you have

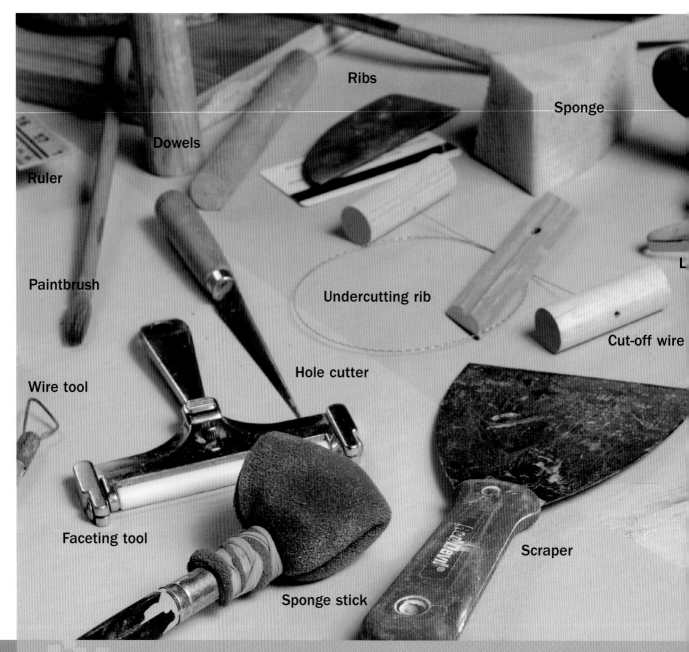

Ribs

Sponge

Dowels

Ruler

Paintbrush

Undercutting rib

L

Cut-off wire

Wire tool

Hole cutter

Faceting tool

Scraper

Sponge stick

favorites—they're the ones that fit your hand in the right way, the ones that work exactly as you want!

Following are general descriptions of the most common tools you'll use when throwing clay. Just keep in mind that the same tool can be used in many different ways. For example, a soft rubber rib will have a different function than one made of steel.

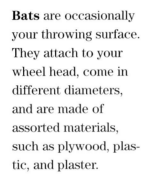

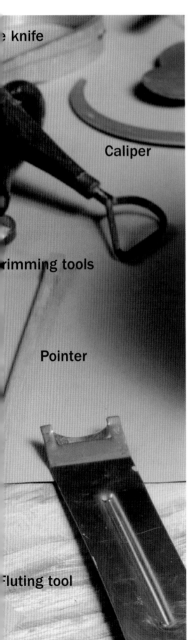

knife

Caliper

rimming tools

Pointer

Fluting tool

Bats are occasionally your throwing surface. They attach to your wheel head, come in different diameters, and are made of assorted materials, such as plywood, plastic, and plaster.

Hole cutters come in different shapes and sizes and are used to cut clean holes in leather-hard clay.

Modeling tools have multiple purposes. You use them when cutting, smoothing, or contouring a piece, or for incising a design or pattern.

Needle tools are pointed needles set in wooden or metal handles. You use them for measuring the thickness of wet clay, trimming a rim, scoring a clay surface, incising patterns, and more.

Looped trimming tools get their name from their pear-shaped blade made of flat, thin, metal ribbons. The tools come in a variety of sizes and shapes and are used for removing clay.

Ribs, either made of rubber, plastic, wood, or metal, are used for shaping a piece as you throw. As the name indicates, this tool evolved from using curved in rib bones to shape the wet clay. You use ribs most commonly to open a form, since they push out a curve. They are also used for smoothing, shaping, and cutting wet clay.

Rulers and calipers measure forms. They help to maintain standard measurements when throwing multiples of one form. Knowing the measurement of a pre-fired form is also key in planning for the shrinkage of the clay.

Sponges keep your clay wet or dry as needed. When throwing, you use them to add or remove water to keep the clay at the right consistency. Sponges also smooth the clay..

Cut-off wires have a length of wire with wooden handles attached to each end. You use the wires to release a form from the bat or wheel head, to section the clay into smaller pieces, and to cut the clay after kneading when testing for air pockets.

Wire tools have wire loops set in wooden handles. The wires come in various shapes and sizes and are used for delicate clay removal, shaping, and sculpting. Double-loop wire tools have loops at both ends of their handles.

There are a myriad of other tools available, each one used to accomplish a specific job. You can find these through clay-supply catalogs, in stores and on-line.

TECHNIQUES

These are the techniques you'll use over and over when making the projects in this book—kneading, centering, opening the clay, pulling a wall, and glazing using wax emulsion. As you continue throwing clay you will become more skilled at each technique. Your willingness to stay with it as you learn will result in your success. Pretty soon it will all be second nature to you, and you'll find that you will move from bowl, to mug, to lidded box with ease.

KNEADING CLAY

I find that kneading clay is a reflective time for me. Aside from the practical labor involved, I'm also connecting with the material that I'll be working with possibly all day or all week. As I push the clay around, I get a sense of it—about its density and its softness. This intimate sense connection provides me with subtle tactile information about the clay that helps me as I throw my forms.

Kneading aligns the particles of the clay to make throwing easier. When you knead, you homogenize the clay by mixing the soft and hard and wet and dry sections together. Most importantly, kneading de-airs the clay. Unlike kneading bread, which is done to mix air into the dough, kneading clay takes the air out.

Following, you'll find descriptions for two different kneading techniques. You'll use the ram's head technique when kneading clay that weighs three pounds or less, and spiral kneading for clay weighing more than three pounds. You want to master at least one of the techniques—if you don't, improper kneading can ruin your project.

Air pockets left in the clay can cause major problems. When throwing the clay, the air pockets will appear as soft bumps on the wall of the pot. When your fingers hit the bumps, they will literally throw your fingers around. This seriously affects the steady pressure you need to apply to the clay and will result in uneven wall thickness and rims that aren't level. When firing the clay, any trapped air

pockets can cause the a form to blow out or blow up. It's just like trapping air in a container—when you heat it, the air expands, causing the container to explode.

You want to knead your clay on a waist-high surface that is clean, dry, and semi-absorbent. Avoid slick surfaces, such as plastic and glass, since the clay will stick to them. It's important to work the clay at waist height—kneading above and below that point, will put undue stress on your body. When you knead, you want to involve your whole body, not just your hands and arms. Position yourself so you are over the clay, not next to it. Use the weight of your upper torso to give your arms and hands power to push through the clay.

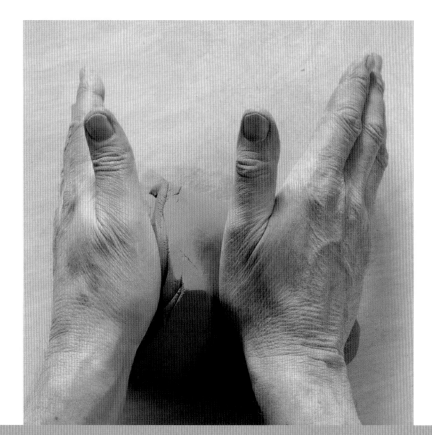

TIPS | DIY Network Crafts

Because you're taking air out of the clay when you're kneading, do not fold the clay at any time during the process. Folding the clay on itself creates pockets that will trap the air.

TESTING FOR AIR POCKETS

Once you complete kneading the clay, you want to test it for air pockets. With the clay still on your work surface, pull a cut-off wire straight through it. If you see divots or open pockets of holes, slap the lump back together and keep kneading!

RAM'S HEAD

This kneading technique works well for clay up to three pounds, or a piece of clay that comfortably fits within two average-sized hands.

1 Place the clay on the kneading surface. Contain the clay from both ends between the palms of your hands. You want to keep your hands parallel—with the palms facing each other—as much as possible throughout the whole process (photo A).

2 With the base of your palms (the fleshy area below the thumbs), push down and slightly across the clay, approximately one-third into the lump. Using a quick repetitive motion, roll the top area of the lump towards you, rotating it one-quarter of a revolution as you do, then pressure into the clay with a quick snap of your wrist. Repeat this sequence 10 to 15 seconds per lump. NOTE: Too much kneading will dry out the clay.

3 After kneading for 10 to 15 seconds, you can see how the rhythm of the method is reflected in the overlapping swirled contours of the clay (photo B).

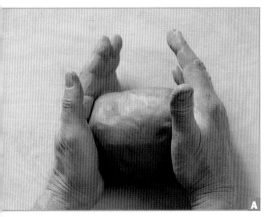

A

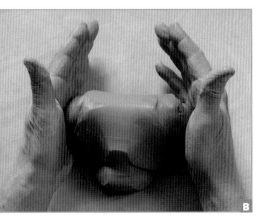

B

TIPS | DIY Network Crafts

It's essential to have a firm, air-free attachment between the clay and the wheel head when throwing clay. You can do this by first making sure the wheel head (or bat) is clean and dry. Then, before placing the clay on the wheel, rotate the base of your kneaded clay on a clean, dry, flat surface to shape the clay into a smooth dome.

SPIRAL KNEADING

This Asian kneading technique is an easier and more manageable method when you have a lump of clay weighing more than three pounds. Since spiral kneading, like the ram's head technique, uses a repetitive motion, you want to add your upper body weight into the mix. Remember to lean over the kneading surface and clay as you work.

1 Place one hand on one end of the clay. Lay the other hand across the top of the clay, keeping the hands near each other.

2 With a quick motion, pressure the palm of the top hand down into the clay and away from you.

3 Using the top hand to assist the hand positioned at the end, roll the top of the clay toward you. As you repeat the motion in steps 2 and 3—push through, pull back, push through, pull back—the clay will rhythmically circulate through your palms.

4 For lumps of clay weighing five pounds or more, let your hands drift during the kneading process to the other end of the lump. Keep in mind that when you're working with these larger lumps, you'll be kneading about one-quarter of the total lump with each repetitive motion (photo A).

5 Much like the ram's head technique, the repetitive motion of spiral kneading will be reflected in the shape of the clay as you work (photo B). You want to knead approximately 10 seconds per five pounds of clay, and 20 seconds for 10 pounds, etc. As you come to the end of your kneading time, shorten the kneading strokes to shape the lump into a compact ball of clay ready for the wheel, or divide the clay into smaller sections.

ARE YOU CENTERED?

If you're a beginner, perform this test to see if your clay is centered. Place one hand with the palm above the clay, allowing the thumb and fingertips of that hand to surround and lightly touch the clay. As the wheel rotates, close your eyes, and let your fingers feel the movement of the clay. If you can feel the clay shaking from left to right and front to back as it rotates, it's not centered.

A

B

CENTERING

Every pot starts with a well-kneaded, centered lump of clay. Centering the clay on the wheel takes practice. It's not something anyone can give you, it's something you must feel. Much like finding your balance when learning to ride a bicycle, you'll know it when it happens!

This process takes some strength, but not an extraordinary amount. It's more about applying smart pressure that will tell you where to push the clay and in what direction. No matter what hand position you use, you always want to apply a firm, constant, steady pressure to the clay. If you apply random pressure, you will not be able to center.

When you center, you want to get your body involved in the process. Use your upper torso. If you don't, you'll find yourself tiring quickly. There is a distinct relationship to the amount of pressure your hands apply to the clay and the speed of the wheel—too little of one or too much of the other and it won't work. Start with a fast wheel speed, but if you feel the clay is out of your control, slow the wheel down.

The clay needs to be very slippery when centering, so use plenty of water during the process. If the clay's surface dries enough to become tacky, the clay will stick to your hands. When this happens, your hands will naturally pull the clay off center.

CENTERING CLAY WEIGHING THREE POUNDS OR LESS

Following are descriptions of different hand positions, each suitable to use when centering clay weighing three pounds or less. Remember to use plenty of water while you center.

Push, Pull, and Top Pressure Position. Cross your thumbs over the clay to connect your hands. Then press inward from both sides and down from the top with both hands using an equal pressure. Once you take your hands away, you can see the pressure points of the hands in the clay.

Pushing Hands Position. Connect your hands at the thumbs in an angel configuration (photo A). Thinking of the wheel as the face of a clock, position your hands at six o'clock. Steadily push the clay away from you toward the center.

Pulling Position. As in the pushing hands position, first connect the hands at the thumbs, then overlap the fingers of each hand. Again, thinking of the wheel as the face of a clock, place the fingers at 12 o'clock and pull clay steadily toward you. Remember to apply steady pressure as you pull (photo B).

One Side and Top Position. Press one hand against the side of the clay with the palm open and the thumb extended toward the ceiling. Since the other hand will pressure the clay downward from the top, position it over the top of the clay and connect the hands at the thumbs (photo C). Use the fingertips of both hands to pressure steadily in and downward at the same time. It helps to lean into the clay with your upper torso. For extra strength as you center, tuck your elbow into the hip that's on the same side of your body as the hand pressing into the side of the clay.

TIPS | DIY Network Crafts

If you're making large, low, wide forms, it helps to use clay that's extra soft. Likewise, use clays that are a bit stiffer for tall forms.

CENTERING CLAY WEIGHING MORE THAN THREE POUNDS

Be patient—centering larger pieces of clay takes longer. You won't necessarily need more strength, but will need to remember to always apply a consistent, steady pressure.

Rough Centering. After attaching the clay to the wheel head, set the wheel at a low speed and repetitively slap the lump into shape (photo A). This process roughly centers the clay.

Pushing Hands Position. Brace your elbows to your lower torso in your hip area. Thinking of the wheel as the face of a clock, spread your hands apart and position them at five and seven o'clock (photo B). With the palms open to the clay, push the clay away from you and towards the center.

Push and Top Pressure Position. This position is similar to the One Side and Top Pressure Position for clay weighing three pounds or less. Position one hand with its palm touching the side of the clay, and the other hand with its palm on the top of the clay. Connect the fingertips and thumbs of the hands wherever possible (photo C). Using both hands, center and use plenty of water.

OPENING CLAY

This step in throwing clay is the beginning of shaping your form. The opening you make enables you to move the centered clay out when making a flat form, or up from the base when making a walled form. Like centering, you'll use different hand positions for different weights of clay. When opening, you want to use a steady, consistent, and gradual force. If you open a piece of clay unevenly, the erratic force will throw even the most perfectly centered piece of clay off center.

Keeping your hands connected through the opening process is essential—one hand will provide stability for the other. If the hands come apart, they'll fly apart independently, making it difficult for you to open the clay. By keeping your hands together, you are creating one stable tool.

OPENING CLAY WEIGHING THREE POUNDS OR LESS

Following is the description of what I call the basic hand position for opening clay. You'll use this position, regardless of whether you go on to make a flat form, bowl shape, or cylinder.

Basic Hand Position. Lock the thumb of one hand into the palm of the other. Place the index finger of one hand over the thumb of the other, then place the middle finger next to the thumb. Keep the tips of the thumb, index, and middle fingers level—you want them to be on the same plane when you open the clay. Keep the gap between the two hands closed and tight (photo A). Take this hand configuration to the centered wet clay. Place the palms of both hands on the clay in the six o'clock position, with the three fingertips at the center. Push down into the center of the clay with the fingertips until you reach your desired base thickness (photo B).

At this stage, you will use different hand positions to continue opening the clay based on whether you are throwing a bowl form or a cylinder or flat form.

Bowl Shape. To open a bowl shape, bend your fingertips and pull them toward you at the five or six o'clock position. Keeping the palms of both hands resting on the thick rim of the spinning clay, use your fingers to slowly draw the clay outward using a steady force. As you draw your fingers outward, gradually relax the downward pressure—this creates the curve of the interior and is the beginning of your bowl form (photo C). Make sure the clay is wet and slippery so you can easily slide your fingers to the center, to the rim, and back to the center, allowing you to compress and shape the interior floor of the bowl form.

Cylinder or Flat Form. To open a cylinder or flat form, push your fingers straight downward into the clay at its center. Keeping your fingertips running parallel to the wheel head, pressure the clay slowly toward the three o'clock position. Use your thumb to force the side of your middle fingertip into the wall to create a tight corner where the base meets the wall (photo D). Forming this inside corner forces the clay into the wall and eventually up into the wall of your pot. This technique is one of the steps to making lightweight pots.

OPENING CLAY WEIGHING THREE POUNDS OR MORE

Using a variation of the basic hand position for centering clay described earlier, take the base of the palm of one hand and steadily push it downward into the center of the wet clay (photo A, left). With fingertips overlapped and palm firmly resting on the thick rim at the six o'clock position, pull the clay slowly toward you, forcing the clay outward. Shape the base until it is the desired form.

PULLING A WALL

The goal for pulling walls is to create a even wall thickness for every pot you make. The average thickness of functionally scaled pots is about ¼". Of course, as you scale-up the size of the pots you make, the walls need to proportionately increase in thickness.

Since clay will wear out as it is worked by the fingertips and become saturated with water, you must plan ahead. Consider the shape, form, finished surface, and any wet decorations before you begin to pull up the wall of your form. Like centering and opening, you will use different hand positions based on the weight of the clay.

PULLING A WALL FOR CLAY WEIGHING THREE POUNDS OR LESS

Since the weight of the clay is less than three pounds, you will use your fingertips to pull a wall. Pulling the walls of a pot using this amount of clay should take four or five pulls.

Fingertip Pulling Position. Distance the middle and ring fingers of both hands from the first and last fingers. Connect the thumb of one hand to the tips of the middle and ring fingers on the same hand. Connect the thumb of the other hand to the middle fingertips of the first hand (photo A, left). These connected digits will sit on the outside of the wall, while the middle and ring finger of the other hand will be the driving force from inside the pot.

To pull the wall upward, first tuck the tip of your thumb under the outside of the form at the base of the wall. Force your thumb under the clay, and then push a groove into the base of the wall (photo B, bottom left). Now tuck your wet middle and ring fingers into the groove beneath the wall. With your other hand inside the pot, fingertips opposite the outside fingertips, slowly pull the clay upward (photo C, right).

When you're finished pulling the wall, you need to level the rim. To do this, position the tip of the index finger of one hand inside the rim and the tip of your thumb outside the rim. Take the index finger of the other hand and bridge the thumb and index finger of the first hand. When you do this, you are basically capturing the rim on the inside, outside, and top (photo D, far right). With your fingers in this position, apply a little pressure to realign the level of the rim.

PULLING A WALL WEIGHING MORE THAN THREE POUNDS

Since our fingertips are quite small in proportion to heavier amounts of clay, we switch hand positions to work more with the palms of the hand and the stronger knuckles. In other words, as you increase the weight, increase the amount of surface contact between the clay and your hands.

Palm Pulling Position. Grasp the wall of clay with one hand, placing your thumb outside and four fingers inside the clay. Rest your palm firmly on the rim. Place the palm of your other hand against the outside wall, covering the thumb. Curl your other thumb over the rim against the inside wall. Push and draw the wall of clay upward and slightly inward (photo A, right).

Knuckle Pulling Position. Since our knuckles are bigger than the pads of our fingers, but smaller than the palms, the knuckle pulling position is used in combination with the fingertip pulling and palm pulling positions. Spread your thumb and first finger, resting them against the wall. With your middle finger knuckle pressed to the wall, opposite the fingertips inside the form, slowly pull the wall upward (photo B, bottom right).

APPLYING WAX EMULSION

You need to apply a wax resist emulsion to the base of most of the pottery you make to prevent the glaze from adhering and then sticking the pot to the kiln shelf. You also apply it between pot and lid fittings to resist the glaze, otherwise, the glaze would fuse them during firing. And, as you'll see throughout the book, you will use wax resist emulsion for decorating between glaze applications.

There are many different types of wax you can use. Some are specific to brush application and decoration, and some are used mostly to coat the bottoms of pots. They come in a wide range of prices. Most are water-based, and will dry within 5 to 10 minutes of application. The emulsion must be dry to the touch before dipping the form in glaze. Most emulsions will need to be are watered down in a 50:50 ratio prior to use.

The tools you'll need for waxing are: wax; three sizes of Japanese calligraphy brushes (the kind with bamboo handles); foam brushes that you can get at any home improvement store; and a banding wheel. The banding wheel is a turntable that allows you to rotate the form as you apply the wax—a smooth-running banding wheel will make for easier decorating. Since waxing is hard on brushes, using inexpensive calligraphy brushes and foam brushes exclusively for waxing is recommended.

WAXING A STRAIGHT LINE

First, make sure your brushes, whether foam or bristle, have a sharp point to ensure a very straight line. Center your pot on a smooth-running banding wheel. Dip the brush in wax. Brace the arm that holds the brush against the table top or your body as you apply the wax—this not only steadies your hand, it steadies your whole thinking process. Apply the wax.

WAXING INSIDE THE RIM

In order to maintain a clear concentric circle of glaze on the inside rim of a pot, you will need to wax inside the rim. Using the same tools and bracing your arm as you did for waxing a straight line, wax a 1" wide band inside and just below the rim (photo A). After dipping the pot upside down into the glaze, you can see how the wax prevented the glaze from getting inside the pot.

DECORATING WITH WAX RESIST

Aside from its practical uses, wax resist emulsion is a wonderful decorating tool for potters. Since water-based glazes will not adhere to waxed surfaces, you can create all manner of interesting designs. When using wax resist for decorating, thin the emulsion with equal parts water for easy and smooth application.

There are two brush-on techniques that you will most commonly use. One is to wax the design directly on bisque-fired pots before dipping the pot in glaze. This step will expose the colored clay body next to the glaze in the final firing. The other technique is waxing patterns between glaze layers giving you a contrast between the first glaze and a second overdipped coat (photo B). For either technique, allow at least 15 minutes for the wax to dry completely before dipping the pot in glaze.

TIPS | DIY Network Crafts

When using a brush with hair bristles, put a dab of dish detergent on the bristles and work it in before dipping the brush in wax. After applying the emulsion, the brush will come completely clean when you wash it with warm water.

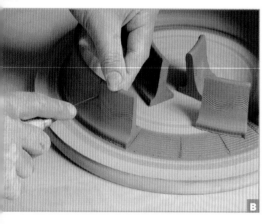

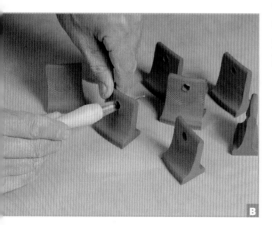

MAKING GLAZE TEST TILES

Test tiles allow you to see how a glaze will look and perform on a specific clay body. Since you create texture on one side of the tiles when you make them, you can also see how the glaze will look when applied to textured surfaces. You want to make the test tiles in quantities in order to have tiles for future testing. When you make the tiles, always use the same clay as the pottery being glazed—it doesn't pay to use a white clay for test tiles if you're using a brown clay for pots.

Since you need to keep track of what you're testing, you'll need to label each tile with a code that you also enter into a book of recipes. You can use a fine tip brush and warm red iron oxide or a ceramic pencil to label the tiles. Or, you can use numbered or lettered stamps to stamp your coding system in the tiles as you make them. If you don't label the tiles, you'll face the worst possible scenario—having great tests come out, but no way of identifying what you did to get them!

WHEEL THROWN TEST TILES

Place four pounds of clay on a bat attached to the wheel head. Throw a short, tapered, bottomless cylinder. Scratch textures on the outside of the ring (photo A). When the rings are leather hard, cut them into 2½" wide sections (photo B). Punch holes near the top of each rim and dry the tiles upright (photo C). The holes allow you to hang the tiles on a wall in your studio or attach them to the handle of a glaze bucket.

EXTRUDED TEST TILES

Extrude hollow lengths or tubes of clay and cut them into uniform pieces. You can extrude the tubes in square, round, or hexagonal shapes (photo A). Each tile should be approximately 3" long. You can make a jig for square-cutting the tubes, or you can use a taut cut-off wire or wire knife (photo B). Impress a stamped texture near the top rim of the tile to show the pooling or breaking effect of a tested glaze (photo C). Punch ample size holes in the tiles. For the ones shown here, I used a ½" cookie cutter in the wall opposite the textured surface. This enables me to hang the tiles from the glaze bucket or mount them on a studio wall (photo D).

TIPS | DIY Network Crafts

If you're waxing a wide band, line the outside edges with wax first. Then, go back and wax between the lines to fill in the area.

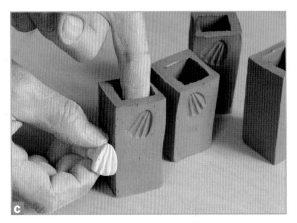

Wheel-Thrown Pottery

2

Starting Projects

No matter how long you've been throwing, the magic of
watching a spinning lump of clay take form never grows
old. Part of the wonder is that basic shapes can be
altered in so many different ways, and that forms can be
combined to create new pieces. In this chapter, you'll
make two variations of the bowl form, the useful mixing
bowl and the elegant fluted bowl with footed base. You'll
learn to make a soup cup and the saucer to go with it.
Then you'll learn to throw low wide forms, otherwise
known as plates. Finally, you'll combine two simple
forms—an inverted bowl over a plate—to make a covered
butter dish.

MIXING BOWL

This handsome bowl combines the simple, curved interior of a basic bowl shape with a spout and handle. I find it's a great addition to any kitchen — you can mix up batter in the bowl and pour it directly onto the griddle, creating a neat and efficient way to make pancakes.

PROJECT SUMMARY

The bowl is the first shape most people learn to throw on the potter's wheel. Often, I throw the bowl in multiple sizes to create a set of graduated mixing bowls. By altering the style of handle I attach to each bowl, the graduated bowls stack inside one another easily. I started this project by first throwing a basic bowl. I stretched the rim to make a spout, then attached a handle opposite to create this visually balanced and useful kitchen tool.

You Will Need

Materials:

- 2-1/2-pound ball of clay for the bowl
- 1-pound ball of clay for the handle
- 2-pound ball of clay for the trimming pad
- Wax-resist emulsion
- Two complementary glazes
- Bucket of water
- Ruler
- Wooden rib
- Soft rubber rib
- Stiff rubber rib
- Looped trimming tool
- Cut-off wire
- Small sponge
- Narrow foam brush
- Small pointed brush
- Signature stamp (optional)

Tools:

- Bat
- Ware boards
- Banding wheel

THROWING THE BOWL

1 To prepare for working at the potter's wheel, weigh out a 2½- pound ball of clay. This amount of clay will make a bowl 4˝ tall and 9˝ across. Knead the clay thoroughly to remove air pockets and homogenize it.

2 Attach a bat to the wheel head. Throwing the bowl on a bat ensures the wet clay can be transferred from the wheel head to the drying rack without being distorted.

3 Rotate the base of the clay ball on a clean, dry surface to make the bottom of the ball smooth. This process makes for a firm, air-free attachment between the clay and the bat (photo A).

4 Using a fast wheel speed, center the ball of clay on the bat. Keep your hands firmly on the clay and your elbows firmly on your thighs or against the wheel tray. The steadier you are in this position, the easier it will be to center the clay (photo B).

5 Next, place your palms and fingers on either side of the clay ball. Cross your thumbs over each other across the top of the clay, then press inward from both sides and down from the top with equal pressure to center the clay. Be sure to use enough water to wet the clay so it slides easily beneath your fingers and palms. If the clay wobbles as the wheel spins, it's not centered. A centered piece of clay will rotate evenly on the wheel head.

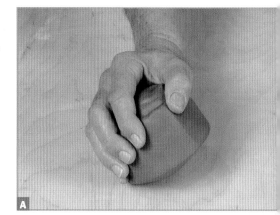

6 The next step is to open the clay. Press the index and middle finger of one hand and the thumb of your other hand into the center of the ball (photo C). Draw your fingertips outward, gradually relaxing the downward pressure. This action gives a curved interior to the form and is the beginning of the bowl shape.

7 Leave a bit less than ½″ of clay between the bat and your fingertips; this is the thickness of the base of the bowl.

8 Now use a needle tool to measure the thickness of the base. First, push the tool into the clay until it touches the wheel head. Next, slide your thumb down the tool until it touches the clay, then remove the tool while keeping your thumb on the mark. The distance between the tip of the tool and your thumb is the thickness of the base.

9 When the base is the right thickness, begin to draw the wall of clay upward. This is called "pulling the wall," and it's a multi-step process that takes several hand positions. It's important to use a medium wheel speed and lots of water while moving the clay upwards. Also, you can slow down the wheel if you feel the clay getting out of your control.

10 To pull the wall of the bowl, first tuck the tip of your thumb under the outside of the form at the base of the wall. Force your thumb under the clay, and then push a groove into the base of the wall (photo D). Now tuck your wet middle and ring fingers into the groove beneath the wall. With your other hand inside the pot, fingertips opposite the outside fingertips, slowly pull the clay upward (photo E).

11 With a ruler, measure the height and diameter of the bowl. Continue to pull and move the clay upwards and slightly outward until the wall measures 4″ high.

12 While pulling, it's better to make the bowl too narrow than too wide. It's easier to stretch the rim outwards to make a slightly larger bowl than to compress the clay to diminish the diameter.

13 Measure the bowl. If it measures less than 9″ across, you'll want to stretch the rim. Wet your hands first so the clay glides easily between your fingertips. Place your fingertips inside and outside the form just below the rim, then gently pull the clay outwards at the 3 o'clock position on the wheel head (photo F). Measure from rim to rim with a ruler, and repeat these steps until you have the right diameter.

14 If the bowl measures more than 9˝ across, compress the wall and rim of the bowl inward. First, wet your hands so the clay slides across your palms and fingertips easily. Place the palms of both hands on the outside of the form at the 12 o'clock position on the wheel head (photo G). With even pressure from both hands, gently press the clay inwards, coaxing the clay towards you. Measure from rim to rim with a ruler, and repeat these steps until the bowl has a 9˝ diameter.

15 When the bowl has the correct dimensions, compress and roll the rim so it is strong, even, and round. Use a slow wheel speed and a very light touch to accomplish this. First, place the thumb tip of your outside hand under the rim of the bowl. With the thumb, index, and middle fingers of your inside hand, roll the clay over your outside thumb tip until the rim thickens and turns round (photo H).

16 The next step is to smooth the inside surface, which also gives a final shape to the interior of the bowl. Placing the curved side of a soft rubber rib at the center of the bowl, move towards the 11 o'clock position on the wheel head. Lightly skim the clay as you move from the center to just below the rim and back. Support the wall of the bowl with your outside hand as you work the rib up and down the inside of the pot (photo I). Make sure to use a very slow wheel speed for this step, and for the other finishing steps that follow.

18 Now smooth the rim with a damp sponge. Wrap the sponge lightly around the rim, smoothing both inside and outside simultaneously.

19 With a wooden rib, make a thin decorative line on the inside of the bowl. Place the tip of the rib just below the rim, pressing very lightly into the clay. Support the outside of the rim with your hand during this step (photo J).

20 With the tip of the wooden rib, cut a beveled groove at the base of the bowl. This groove is a guide for the cut-off wire and helps to free the pot cleanly and evenly from the bat (photo K).

TIPS | DIY Network Crafts

To make a graduated, or nesting, set of bowls start with a 1-pound ball of clay. Add 12 ounces of clay for each larger sized bowl you want to throw on the wheel.

◢◢◢ MAKING THE SPOUT ◢◢◢

1 The next step is to create the spout at the rim of the bowl. First, stop the wheel and wet the rim of the bowl where you're going to make the spout. Wet the fingertips and thumb of one hand. Slide your wet fingers back and forth three or four times across the dampened rim to stretch the clay outward. Use a sponge to remove the slip and smooth the edge of the spout.

2 With dry hands, place the thumb and index finger of one hand at either side of the flattened edge of the rim (photo A). Wet the index finger of your other hand and slide it back and forth on the wet, stretched rim, pressing down on the clay to form the spout (photo B). Crease the corners of the spout so liquids will flow smoothly out of the bowl (photo C).

3 With a taught cut-off wire, release the bowl from the bat. Place the wire into the beveled groove at the base of the bowl, then pull it evenly to ensure a level cut. Remove the bat from the wheel head.

4 Set the bowl aside to dry until it is leather hard. A leather-hard pot will feel like hard cheddar cheese — stiff, but still pliable. Drying time depends on humidity and the conditions of your studio. You can accelerate the drying process by placing pots in front of a fan or under a heat lamp.

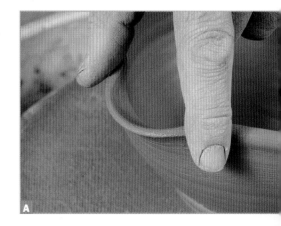

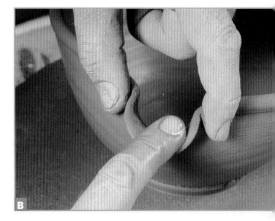

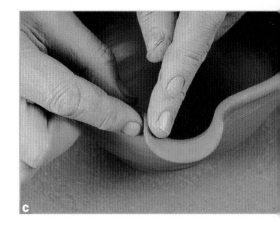

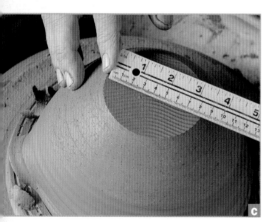

◢◣ TRIMMING THE BOWL ◢◣

1 When the bowl is leather hard, it's ready to trim. When you are learning to throw, the bottom section of the pulled wall is often thicker than the top section. To correct this, you can trim up the side of the bowl as far as necessary to make the wall an even thickness. To keep from damaging the spout, trim the bowl on a clay or foam rubber pad.

2 To make a clay trimming pad, center a 2-pound ball of clay directly on the wheel head. Open the clay until the diameter is slightly larger than the top of the bowl, and make sure the surface is level. Skim the surface with a stiff rubber rib, removing the slip and excess water. With the tip of your finger or a wooden rib, mark several concentric circles in the pad. These circles are guidelines that assist in centering the pot on the pad (photo A).

3 Invert the bowl and center it on the trimming pad. Press down on it gently to ensure a strong attachment between the rim of the bowl and the pad.

4 With a looped trimming tool and a quick wheel speed, carve away the excess clay from the wall until it's a little less than ¼˝ thick (photo B). The profile of the bowl will change as it's trimmed. Aim for a gentle curve from the base to the rim.

5 As a general rule, the diameter of the base should be one-third the diameter of the bowl. In this case, the base will measure about 3˝ across (photo C).

6 Trim a narrow bevel at the edge of the base. With the tip of your finger or the flat surface of a soft rubber rib, push the aggregate (the sand) raised by the trimming tool back into the beveled surface.

7 Dampen the trimmed wall with a soft sponge. Burnish and smooth the trimmed surface with a soft rubber rib or with the tip of your finger. Then push in gently at the center of the bottom of the bowl. This depression prevents the base from bulging out as it dries.

8 Sign the underside of the bowl or use your signature stamp somewhere on or near the base (photo D). Release the bowl from the trimming pad, then make sure the rim is clean and dry before setting the bowl aside.

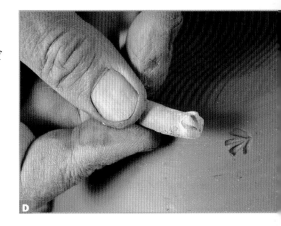

◢◢ MAKING THE HANDLE ▮▮▶

1 The next step is to make a handle and attach it to the bowl. To begin, prepare a dry space on which to work.

2 Pulling a handle is a multi-step process. First, form a carrot shape with a pound of kneaded clay (photo A). Holding the carrot in one hand, dip the bottom in water.

3 Stretch the wet clay with your other hand, drawing the clay downward as you stroke it (photo B). Rotate the carrot several times as you pull the clay downwards to create an even cross section. The handle "blank" should be about 1¼" wide — or about the same width as the spout — and 4" long.

4 If possible, pull all the handles for your graduated mixing bowls at the same time.

Generally, a 1-pound ball of clay yields six handle blanks.

5 With the tip of your thumb or your thumbnail, create two decorative grooves on the front of the handle blank you have made. Support the back of the handle with your fingers as you make the groove (photo C).

6 Pinch off the handle blank from the carrot-shaped clay. Place it on a clean, dry surface (photo D).

7 To attach the handle, make a small mark with your fingernail directly across from the center of the spout. This spot is where the top of the handle will be attached to the bowl. Make sure your hands are dry before you attach the handle or it will stick to your fingers.

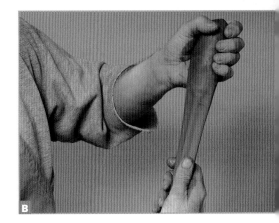

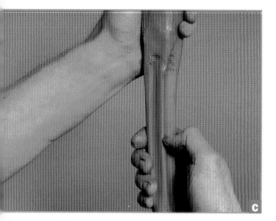

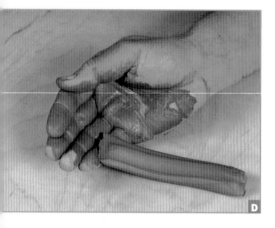

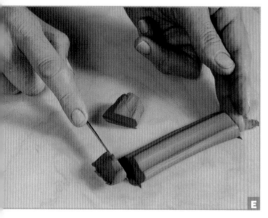

8 Now trim the ends of the handle blank with a fettling knife (photo E). With a damp sponge, wet the area near the rim where you'll attach the handle. Let the water soak into the surface until it's sticky.

9 Wet one end of the blank and let the water soak into the surface. Support the rim with one hand inside the bowl, and then press the wet end of the blank firmly into place just below the rim. Don't be afraid to really force the clay onto the wall of the pot for a firm attachment.

10 With the tip of your thumb, press lightly to smooth the area where the handle attaches to the rim. Don't smear the clay but keep the joint visible.

11 Pick the bowl up with one hand. The handle blank should hang straight down.

12 With slightly damp fingers, continue to pull the handle, stretching the clay until the blank is 6˝ long. Make sure to pull the blank straight down or the handle will be lopsided.

13 With a damp sponge, wet the bowl where the bottom of the handle will be attached. Let the water soak into the wall of the pot for a few seconds.

14 While carefully holding on to the end of the handle, turn the bowl until it's horizontal. Then stick the end of the handle to the side of the bowl.

TIPS | DIY Network Crafts

As you prepare the clay to be used to make your bowl, establish the details in your mind's eye. What dimensions will it have? What rim shape will be used at the edge of the bowl? What will the base, or foot of the bowl look like? Some preplanning keeps the throwing steps organized and allows you to efficiently work.

15 Set the bowl down. Press the end of the handle firmly to the bowl while supporting the inside wall with one hand.

16 Adjust the shape of the handle. First, look through it to assess the shape, then run a damp finger inside the handle, lifting and stretching it upward slightly to create a graceful, curved profile (photo G).

17 With a damp sponge, smooth the joint area where the handle attaches to the bowl. If you miss this step, the edges of the joint become razor sharp once they're fired and glazed.

18 Set the bowl aside on a clean wareboard. Let the bowl air-dry until it is bone dry. If the bowl feels damp or cool to the touch, it's still not bone dry.

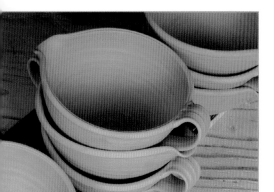

▲▌▎ FIRING, WAXING, & GLAZING ▎▌▲

1 Bisque fire the bowl in the kiln to approximately 1750° Fahrenheit for about 10 to 12 hours (photo A). When the bisque kiln has cooled to 200° Fahrenheit, it's ready to open.

2 To glaze the mixing bowl, select two complementary glaze colors.

3 With a narrow foam brush, apply wax-resist emulsion to the base of the bowl. Wax at least ¼″ up the wall of the bowl.

4 Rotating the bowl on a banding wheel while applying the wax emulsion guarantees an even wax line. To prevent damaging the spout, place the bowl upside down on a thick foam pad, or balance it on another pot to elevate the rim from the banding wheel (photo B).

5 Set the bowl aside to dry for about 10 minutes. The wax emulsion should be dry to the touch before dipping the bowl in the glaze.

6 Stir the first glaze to mix up any particles that may have settled to the bottom. Dip the bowl in the first glaze while holding onto the rim, keeping the pot submerged for three seconds (photo C).

7 Place the bowl on a clean wareboard. Immediately touch up the rim where you held the pot during the dip. Use your finger or a small, soft brush to dab glaze over the bare clay (photo D).

8 When the sheen has gone off the bowl, the first layer of glaze is dry. Clean the waxed area with a damp sponge to remove any excess glaze beads that might have adhered to the waxed base.

9 Stir the second glaze thoroughly. Holding the rim and the base of the bowl, dip one side of the bowl into the second glaze. This is a very quick dip — no more than one or two seconds (photo E).

10 Set the bowl aside on a clean wareboard until the second layer of glaze is dry. The second dip will take longer to dry than the first.

11 Place the bowl into the kiln for the glaze firing. The kiln should fire to Cone 6, or about 2200° Fahrenheit, for about 10 to 12 hours. Let the kiln cool for an additional 36 hours before unloading it.

12 Take your mixing bowl to the kitchen and have fun!

Mixing Bowl Glaze Recipe

The primary glaze is Nutmeg. It's an opaque semi-matte glaze fired to cone 6 in oxidation. The secondary glaze is Waxy White and is also fired to cone 6 in oxidation.

NUTMEG:		WAXY WHITE:	
Dolomite	23.3%	Custer Feldspar	62.0 %
Spodumene (Australian)	23.3%	Whiting	14.0 %
OM #4 Ball Clay	23.3%	Talc	8.0 %
Silica	23.3%	Kaolin (EPK)	10.0 %
Ferro Frit #3134	6.8%	Zinc Oxide	6.0 %
	100.0%		100.0 %

ADD:	
Red Iron Oxide	1.07%
Yellow Ochre	3.24%
Tin Oxide	4.85%
Bentonite	1.90%

LUG HANDLE

A number of handle styles work well with this versatile mixing bowl. I attach lug handles when I throw a graduated set of mixing bowls so they will nest inside of each other easily.

1 To make a lug handle, first prepare a clean, dry table on which to work. Form a 1-pound piece of kneaded clay into a fat, coiled carrot shape.

2 Hold the top of the carrot in one hand and dip three-fourths of it into a bucket of water. With your other hand, stretch and draw the wet clay downwards as you stroke it (photo A).

3 Rotate the carrot several times as you pull the clay downward to create an even cross section and rounded edges. The handle should be about 1″ wide — or a bit narrower than the width of the spout — and about 4″ to 5″ long.

4 With the tip of your thumb or your thumbnail, create two grooves on the front of the handle. Make one groove shallow and the other deep. The deeper groove will make one edge of the handle thinner than the other. Support the back of the handle with your fingers as you make the grooves (photo B).

5 Pinch off the handle from the carrot-shaped clay and place it on a clean, dry surface.

6 To position the lug handle, mark a place just below the rim and directly across from the center of the spout (photo C). Make sure your hands are dry before you attach the handle or it will stick to your fingers.

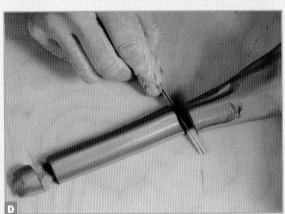

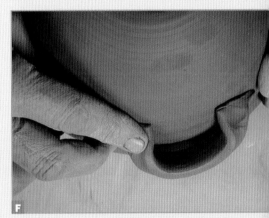

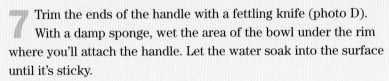

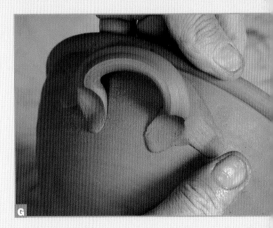

7 Trim the ends of the handle with a fettling knife (photo D). With a damp sponge, wet the area of the bowl under the rim where you'll attach the handle. Let the water soak into the surface until it's sticky.

8 With a damp sponge, wet the underside of the handle. Let the water soak into the surface.

9 Invert the bowl on a clean surface. Attach the thin side of the handle to the bowl just below the rim, using the mark to center it (photo E). Bend the ends of the handle inward and under the handle (photo F). Remove the excess clay.

10 Secure the ends tightly to the wall of the bowl with your thumb (photo G), supporting the wall from the inside as you work. Slide a wet fingertip back and forth underneath the handle, stretching it upward to make the handle easy to grasp and use.

11 With a damp sponge, lightly smooth over the handle and the area where it attaches to the side of the bowl.

FLUTED BOWL

This bowl is a sophisticated centerpiece for any dining table, mantelpiece, or coffee table. But being refined doesn't make it any less practical; it can be filled with salad, pinecones, or floating flowers to suit whatever occasions arise.

▥ PROJECT SUMMARY ▥

Expanding on the basic bowl shape is easy, and it's a good step in building your repertoire as a potter. This beautiful bowl is quite simple to make. I've combined basic throwing techniques with a specialized tool to create a piece with an unusual decorative element — scalloped flutes. These flutes give the bowl a graceful look. And by selecting contrasting yet complementary glazes, the flutes are highlighted in the finished piece. Elevating the bowl with a raised foot adds to its overall elegance.

You Will Need

Materials:

- 8 pounds of soft clay
- Wax-resist emulsion
- Two contrasting yet complementary glazes
- Bucket of water

Tools:

- Large bat
- Banding wheel
- Foam trimming pad (preferably attached to a bat)
- Ruler
- Fluting tool
- Undercutting rib
- Wooden rib
- Soft rubber rib
- Stiff rubber rib
- Looped trimming tool
- Cut-off wire
- Nylon sanding pad
- Dust mask
- Small sponge
- Soft bristled brush
- Narrow foam brush
- Small pointed brush
- Signature stamp (optional)

THROWING THE BOWL

1 To prepare for throwing the bowl on the potter's wheel, weigh out 8 pounds of very soft clay. Divide the clay into two lumps of 4 pounds each. Knead each lump thoroughly to remove air pockets and homogenize the clay.

2 Press and rotate one lump of clay on a clean, dry, and flat surface to produce a smooth, domed base (photo A). Repeat this step with the other lump of clay.

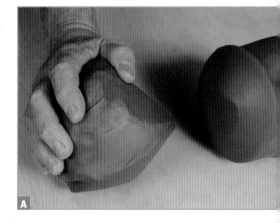

A

3 Attach a large bat to the wheel head. Throwing a large form on a bat allows you to easily transfer the wet piece from the wheel head to the drying rack without warping or distorting it.

4 Next, you'll center the clay using a fast wheel speed. Place one 4-pound lump of clay on the wheel head, domed side down. Center the clay, using enough water so the clay glides easily beneath your palms and fingers.

5 With a stiff rubber rib, smooth the top of the clay to form a domed surface. Be sure to remove all of the slip from the surface with the rib (photo B).

B

6 Slap the second lump of clay, domed surface down, on top of the centered lump of clay (photo C). Using plenty of water, center the second lump of clay on top of the first. The two 4-pound pieces should blend together to form one large lump of centered clay.

7 Now the clay is ready to open. Press the index, middle, and ring fingers of one hand and the thumb of your other hand down into the center of the clay (photo D).

8 Draw your hands outward, leaving about 1˝ of clay between the wheel head and your fingertips. It's necessary to leave this much clay at the base in order to trim a tall foot under the bowl later.

9 To measure the thickness of the base, first stop the wheel. Poke the end of a needle tool into the center of the base until it touches the wheel head. Slide the tip of your thumb down the tool until it touches the clay. Remove the tool while keeping your thumb on the mark, then measure the distance between the end of the tool and your thumb.

10 As you continue to open the clay, begin to form the curved interior of the bowl by relaxing your fingers as you draw them outward. Varying the pressure between the center of the clay and the outer half of the short cylinder forms the inside curve at the bottom of the bowl (photo E).

11 Measure the form. Once the low, wide cylinder is open, the inside base should be about 8˝ in diameter.

12 Next, begin to draw the wall of clay upward. Use a medium wheel speed and lots of water to move the clay from the base to the rim. If the clay feels like it's getting out of control, decrease the wheel speed.

13 Pulling the wall of this 8-pound bowl is different than pulling the wall of an average bowl — it requires a few specific hand positions. First, grasp the wall of clay with one hand, placing the thumb outside the bowl and four fingers on the inside. Rest your palm firmly on the rim (photo F).

14 Now place the palm of your other hand against the outside wall, covering the thumb. Curl your other thumb over the rim against the inside wall (photo G). Then push and draw the wall of clay upward and slightly inward. Use this hand position two or three times until the wall of the bowl is about 4″ tall.

15 Now change hand positions to refine and complete pulling the wall. Force the tip of your thumb under the clay to push a groove into the base of the wall. Tuck the middle, ring, and pinky fingers of your outside hand into the groove, and then slide the clay upward from the base to the rim.

16 Keep your hands connected during this process and use plenty of water. Position your other hand inside the pot, fingertips opposite your outside fingertips, as you pull the clay upward (photo H).

17 The wall should be about 5″ tall and ½″ thick, or twice as thick as the wall of a normal pot. Since half of the wall's thickness will be removed with the fluting tool, it's crucial to make a thick wall now.

18 The wall of the finished bowl will be straight, so make the remaining pulls up — rather than up and out — once the curved base inside the bowl is established (photo I).

19 To counteract the clay's tendency to flair out as it spins on the wheel head, use more pressure with the outside hand while relaxing the inside hand as you pull the wall. This action curves the wall slightly inward at the rim.

20 Keep the palm of your inside hand resting firmly on the rim as you pull the wall upward; this hand position helps to keep the rim level. When the rim of a pot is under control, it's easier to control the whole form (photo J).

21 With a ruler, measure the diameter of the bowl. It should now be about 9˝ from outside edge to outside edge. If the diameter of the bowl is too small, expand it as you pull the wall upward. To do this, firmly press the wall with your inside fingers as you make each pull, stretching the clay outward as you pull from base to rim (photo K). Work slowly and methodically; don't try to increase the diameter of the bowl in one pull. Move the clay outward and upward until the diameter is right.

22 Fluting works best on a smooth surface, so it's important to finish the outside wall very evenly. There are several steps to creating a smooth surface. First, make the last few pulls on the bowl with the knuckles of your outside hand instead of with your fingertips (photo L). Then place the long, straight side of a rib on the outside wall. Push the clay against the rib with your inside fingertips as you run the rib up and down the outside of the wall (photo M).

23 Remove any excess water and slip from inside the bowl with a sponge, then clean up the outside base of the bowl with the rubber rib (photo N). Smooth the inside surface of the bowl with a soft rubber rib.

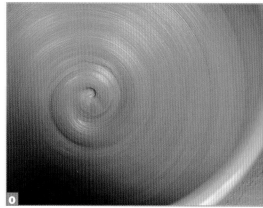

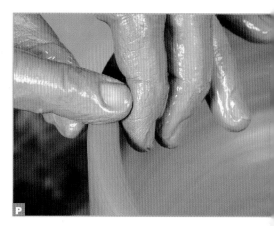

24 To add visual movement, place a swirl inside the center of the bowl. With a fingertip or the side of your thumb, press down slightly as you slide from outside to center in one quick motion (photo O).

25 To prepare for fluting, the outside edge of the rim must be square. First place one fingertip across the rim, a thumb tip on the outside of the rim, and a fingertip inside the rim. Press the fingertips and thumb tip together at a 90° angle until the rim forms a square edge (photo P). Soften the inside of the rim with a damp sponge until it forms a gentle, round curve.

26 Cut a groove at the base, or foot, of the bowl with the tip of a wooden rib or an undercutting rib (photo Q). This will make cutting the bowl from the bat easier.

27 Now stop the wheel. Place a cut-off wire in the groove at the foot of the bowl, then pull it under in one fluid motion to separate the bowl from the bat. Leave the bowl on the bat; if you try to pick it up now it will collapse.

28 Set the bowl aside to air-dry until it's soft-leather hard. Soft-leather hard means the clay still bends, but it's not tacky to the touch. If the bowl is too stiff, the clay will tear as it's fluted.

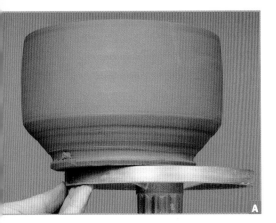

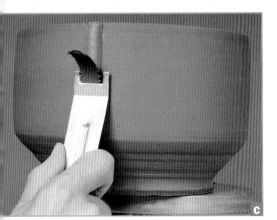

▚▚ FLUTING ▚▚

1 The next step is fluting the outside wall of the bowl. Place the bowl off-center on a banding wheel so the base hangs over the edge (photo A). It's best to flute at eye level, so elevate the banding wheel or sit down, or both.

2 All of the flutes follow this initial cut, so it's important to get it right the first time. Place the U-shaped band of the fluting tool on top of the rim. The wings on the side of the tool keep it from cutting too deeply into the side of the bowl (photo B).

3 With a smooth, slow stroke, pull the fluting tool from the rim to the base of the bowl. If the bowl is placed properly on the banding wheel, there should be enough room to pull straight through the wall of the bowl in a single motion (photo C).

4 Proper tool placement is essential for the flutes to have a clean, crisp edge. A flat wall surface will show between the flutes if the tool is placed incorrectly.

5 Place the fluting tool on top of the rim for the next cut. The tool should overlap the last cut slightly. Line up the tool so that the U-shaped cutting blade aligns with the right edge of the flute that was just cut (photo D). Slowly pull the fluting tool from the rim to the base with one smooth stroke.

6 Place the tool on top of the rim again, aligning the tool with the right edge of the last flute. Again, pull the tool from rim to base with one stroke.

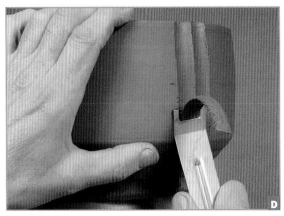

7 Turn the banding wheel as needed so the area to be fluted is always directly in front of you. Work around the bowl slowly, steadily, and with patience; a bad cut is almost impossible to repair.

8 When the outside is fluted all the way around, set the bowl aside to air-dry until the base is stiff-leather hard (photo E). Don't try to remove the burrs created by the fluting tool now. They'll be sanded away when the bowl is bone dry.

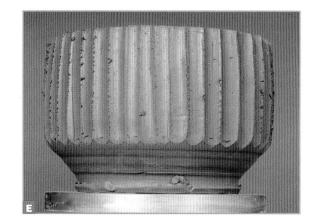

⫶⫶⫶ TRIMMING ⫶⫶⫶

1 To trim the bowl, invert it on a thick foam pad on the wheel head. With a very quick wheel speed and a looped trimming tool, remove the excess clay from the bottom of the bowl.

2 To get the best results while trimming, use the wide, curved end and the longer edge of the looped trimming tool to do most of the trimming. Keep both hands connected to the tool at all times to keep it steady; a stable hand position yields an even, smooth trimmed surface.

3 To keep the bowl firmly in place on the foam pad, press down on the base with the fingers of one hand as you trim.

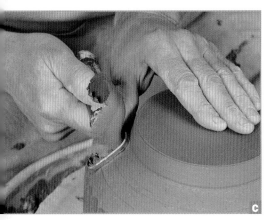

MAKING THE FOOT RING

1 Now you'll define the foot ring. The diameter of the foot should be about half the total diameter of the bowl, or about 4˝ to 5˝. This classical proportion suits this formal piece of pottery.

2 Measure the base with a ruler. Then, with the wheel spinning slowly, make a circular mark with your fingernail to indicate the outside edge of the foot ring.

3 Next, trim away the excess clay until the surface between the circular mark and the bottom edge of the flutes is smooth and even, with a gradual slope (photo A). Use the wide, round end of the loop tool first, then use the long edge of the blade to finish trimming. Move from inside to outside as you work, from the foot to the edge of the flutes. Measure again to make sure the diameter of the foot is correct.

4 Now create an elevated base for the bowl by trimming a tall foot. First, trim and shape the outside edge of the foot by placing the narrow end of the tool flush against the outside edge of the foot (photo B). Gently press down to remove the excess clay. When finished, the outside wall of the foot should be about 1˝ tall (photo C).

5 With the long edge of the tool, trim and define the slope between the foot and the base of the flutes.

6 To accentuate the foot, use the narrow end of the trimming tool to cut a small groove where the top of the foot meets the bottom of the slope. This creates a shadow that highlights the elegant lift of the elevated bowl (photo D).

7 To finish the tall foot, measure about ¼″ in from the outside edge. With the wheel spinning, mark a second circle with your fingernail. This is the inside edge of the foot. Place the narrow end of the loop tool on the mark you just made, then gently press down with the tip to create a deep cut parallel to the outside wall of the foot (photo E).

8 With the width and depth of the foot established, remove the excess clay inside the foot. Trim from center toward the foot with the long edge of the tool.

9 Overall, the bottom should be about ¼″ thick, or the same thickness as the wall of the fluted bowl.

10 To curve the base inside the tall foot so it mirrors the interior curve of the bowl, press down firmly with the tool as you trim from center to the foot ring.

11 It's important to make the base an even thickness so the bowl doesn't crack as it dries. Pick up the bowl periodically to test the weight.

12 Bevel the inside and outside edges of the foot ring (photo F), then smooth the bevels with your fingertip when finished. Roll a fingertip back and forth over the foot ring to push the aggregate (or sand) back into the clay.

13 Dampen all of the trimmed areas with a sponge, excluding the foot ring. Burnish the damp surfaces with a soft rubber rib or your fingertip.

14 Sign the bowl or use your signature stamp inside the foot ring, or on the bottom near the base of the flutes (photo G). Set the bowl aside to dry until it's bone dry.

15 Once the bowl is bone dry, you're ready to sand the flutes. Put on a dust mask, then lightly sand the flutes with a nylon sanding pad to remove burrs left by the fluting tool. Sweep out the dust between the flutes and inside the bowl with a soft brush.

E

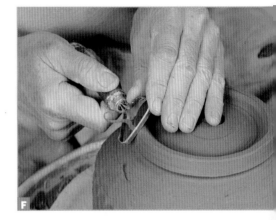

F

G

▐▐▐▐ FIRING, WAXING, & GLAZING ▐▐▐▐

1 Place the bowl into the kiln for the first firing. Fire the bisque kiln to approximately 1750° Fahrenheit for about 10 to 12 hours. When the bisque kiln has cooled to 200° Fahrenheit or less, it's ready to open.

2 Invert the bowl on a banding wheel to apply wax-resist emulsion. Rotating the bowl on a banding wheel while waxing ensures a neat, even wax line.

3 Use a narrow foam brush to apply wax-resist emulsion to the foot ring. Wax about ¼″ up the tall foot inside and out (photo A), then set the bowl aside to dry for about 10 minutes. The wax emulsion should be dry to the touch before proceeding.

4 To glaze the bowl, select two contrasting yet complementary glaze colors. Stir the first glaze to mix up any particles that may have settled to the bottom. This is the base glaze, and it will coat the bowl inside and out.

5 Dip the bowl in the first glaze, holding it at the rim and the waxed foot. Keep the pot submerged for about three seconds. Place the bowl upright on the banding wheel, then immediately touch up the rim where you held the bowl during the dip. Use your finger or a small, soft brush to dab glaze over the bare clay (photo B).

6 When the sheen has gone off the bowl, the first layer of glaze is dry. Clean the foot ring with a damp sponge to remove any excess glaze beads that might have adhered to the waxed surface (photo C).

7 Stir the second glaze thoroughly. This is the accent glaze, and it will coat the flutes on the outside of the bowl. Hold the bowl by the foot, then dip it into the glaze rim first for about two seconds, covering about 1″ past the bottom of the fluted surface for an aesthetically pleasing result (photo D). Keep the bowl level as you dip it into the glaze; the air trapped inside the bowl will prevent the glaze from entering and coating the interior unevenly.

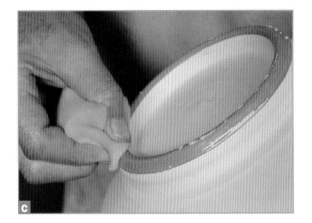

8 Let the bowl dry upside down for a minute or so over the glaze bucket before turning it upright. This prevents glaze drips and runs on the outside of the bowl.

9 Place the bowl on a clean, dry surface free of glaze. Let the bowl air-dry completely, which takes about 10 or 15 minutes.

10 Place the bowl into the kiln for the glaze firing. The kiln should fire to cone 6, or about 2200° Fahrenheit, for about 10 to 12 hours. Let the kiln cool for an additional 36 hours before unloading it.

TIPS | DIY Network Crafts

Making your own faceting tool is fairly simple. Purchase an adjustable metal cheese-slicer, usually available in supermarkets and kitchen stores. Apply a dab of epoxy to each end of the roller to fix it in place permanently. Remove the cheese-slicer's thick wire and replace it with a taught wire of your choice (photo at right).

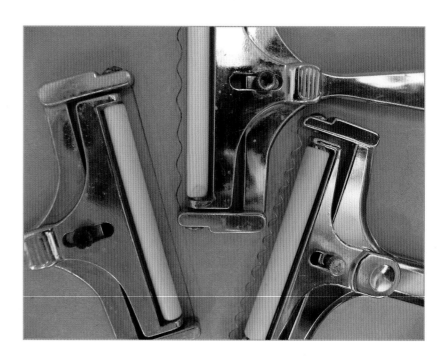

Fluted Bowl Glaze Recipe

The primary glaze is Teal Blue. It's fired to cone 6 in oxidation. The secondary glaze is Rutile Green. It's glossy, and great as a thin over-dip on all cone 6 glazes.

TEAL BLUE:		RUTIILE GREEN:	
Custer Feldspar	20%	Talc	5.0%
Ferro Frit #3124	20%	Custer Feldspar	22.0%
Wollastonite	20%	Whiting	4.0%
Silica	20%	Silica	26.0%
EPK	20%	Tile #6 or EPK	17.0%
	100%	Ferro Frit #3134	26.0%
ADD:			100.0%
Cobalt Carbonate	1.0%	**ADD:**	
Chrome Oxide	0.5%	Bentonite	2.0%
		Rutile (powdered)	6.0%
		Copper Carbonate	4.0%

FACETING BOWLS

1 Position the faceting tool at the base of the bowl with the wire below the wall and the roller contacting the side of the bowl (photo A).

2 Firmly pull the cutting wire up and through the wall. The wire will exit through the rim, bisecting the rim and cutting away the outer half of the wall.

3 Remove the clay from the outer half of the wall if it doesn't just peel away with the tool (photo B).

4 Reposition the wire below the base of the wall to the right of the first facet, overlapping one end of the wire about ¼″ into the facet that's already been cut. Again, firmly pull the wire up and through the wall (photo C).

5 Repeat steps 1 through 4. Work around the bowl, with rhythm, until you reach the first facet you cut. The final cut will join the last facet to the first. Don't leave any wall surface showing between the facets (photo D).

SOUP CUP & SAUCER

For this project, I've paired the flat form of a shallow plate with a small, deep bowl to create a versatile soup cup and saucer. It's a great matched set; the saucer is tailor-made to the cup with a center well that fits the cup's foot perfectly.

▟▟ **PROJECT SUMMARY** ▙▙

I throw the bowl first and then the shallow plate. Next, I define the well of the saucer, then trim the foot of the cup to fit the well. The handle is thrown off the hump. When I put it all together, I've got a functional favorite that'll never go out of style.

The set can be made in a traditional style, or it can be made more unusual depending on the design of the handle attached to the cup. I prefer this European style of handle. It's sturdy, easy to use, and interesting to throw. I've added a personal flair by painting a lively decoration with wax between the two layers of glaze.

You Will Need

Materials:

- 1 pound 4 ounce ball of clay (for the cup)
- 2-pound ball of clay (for the saucer)
- 1-pound ball of clay (for the handle)
- 1-pound ball of clay (for the trimming pad)
- Wax-resist emulsion
- Bucket of water
- Two contrasting glazes

Tools:

- Small bat
- Banding wheel
- Ruler
- Undercutting rib
- Wooden rib
- Soft rubber rib
- Stiff rubber rib
- Looped trimming tool
- Cut-off wire
- Small sponge
- Narrow foam brush
- Two fine-tipped brushes
- Signature stamp (optional)

THROWING THE CUP

1 To prepare for throwing at the potter's wheel, weigh out three lumps of clay: one ball of clay 1 pound 4 ounces, one 2-pound ball, and one 1-pound ball. Knead the clay thoroughly to remove air pockets.

2 Throw the cup using the 1 pound 4 ounce ball of clay. The cup will be 3½″ high and 5½″ in diameter. It can be thrown directly on the wheel head without a bat because a piece this size and shape can be picked up — if you're careful — without being distorted.

3 Center the clay using a fast wheel speed and plenty of water so the clay slides easily beneath your palms and fingers. Open the clay by pressing the index and middle fingers of one hand and the thumb of your other hand downward into the center of the clay (photo A).

4 Draw your hands and fingertips outward and toward you. Begin to form the curved interior of the cup by relaxing your fingertips as you draw them toward the edge of the clay. Leave a little more than ¼″ between the wheel head and your fingertips so you can trim a raised foot at the base of the cup later.

5 To measure the thickness of the base, first stop the wheel. Poke the end of a needle tool into the base until it touches the wheel head. Slide the tip of your thumb down the tool until it touches the clay.

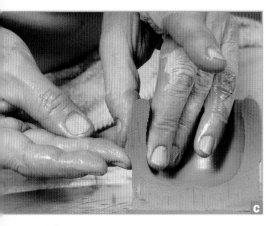

6 Remove the tool while keeping your thumb on the mark, then measure the distance between the sharp end of the tool and your thumb tip.

7 Next, pull the wall of the cup up and slightly outward. To pull the wall upward, first tuck a thumb tip under the outside of the form at the base of the wall. Press the tip of your thumb into and under the clay to push a groove into the base area (photo B).

8 Tuck your middle and ring fingers into the groove, then slide the clay upward from the base to the rim. Keep the fingertips of your other hand inside the pot, opposite the outside fingertips, as you pull the clay upward (photo C).

9 The wall of the cup should be about ¼˝ thick. After three or four complete pulls, use a ruler to measure the height and diameter of the cup. Make the necessary adjustments to the cup's size as you

make the last couple of pulls. If both the height and diameter of the cup are too small, gently coax the wall outward as you pull it up.

10 If the height is right but the diameter is too small, place your hands at the 3 o'clock position on the wheel head. Place the index and middle fingers of one hand inside the cup. The index and middle fingertips of the other hand should be placed opposite on the outside wall. Keep your hands connected above the rim for stability.

11 Gently stretch the wall outward as you move your fingertips upward until the diameter is right. Try not to change the shape of the cup too much as you adjust the width. The widest point across the cup is at its belly, about 1˝ below the rim. As you widen the diameter of the rim, some minor adjustment to the width of the belly may also be necessary.

12 If the height is right but the diameter is too big, place your palms flat against the outside of the wall at the 12 o'clock position on the wheel head; gently press inward until the diameter is right. If needed, adjust the diameter and shape of the belly to retain a rounded form.

13 Use the straight edge of a wooden rib or the side of an undercutting rib to give the cup its final shape. First, place the rib on the outside of the wall. Then place your other hand inside the cup, fingertips opposite the rib. Keep your hands connected above the rim while you work.

14 Run the rib up and down the wall, gently pressing the rib into the clay and against your inside fingertips. This action removes the slip from the surface and smoothes the wall.

15 Press outward slightly with your fingertips to give the cup a well-defined, rounded belly (photo D). Then press inward slightly with the rib at the rim to give the cup its final, graceful shape (photo E).

16 With the tip of an undercutting rib, cut a beveled groove about ½″ deep at the base of the cup.

17 To create a cup that's comfortable to drink from, bevel the inside edge of the rim. Begin by placing the straight edge of a wooden rib or the side of an undercutting rib against the inside edge of the rim. Support the rim on the outside with a damp finger placed opposite the tool.

18 Press the tool lightly into the clay to form a beveled inner rim with a gentle slope (photo F), then soften the rim with a damp sponge. Be careful not to make the edge of the rim too sharp or it'll chip easily.

19 Wrap the sponge around the rim as the cup makes several revolutions on the wheel (photo G).

20 Place a cut-off wire in the groove at the cup's foot. With the wheel spinning, pull the wire under the cup to free it from the wheel head.

21 Stop the wheel and dry your hands. Place all of your fingertips into the beveled groove at the base of the cup. Starting at the 12 o'clock position on the wheel, pry up the edge of the cup and gently maneuver your fingertips under the base (photo H). Try not to touch the wall as you remove the cup from the wheel head and place it gently on the wareboard (photo I).

THROWING THE SAUCER

1 Next, you'll throw the saucer. Since it's difficult to lift a low, wide form from the wheel head when it's wet, begin by attaching a bat onto the wheel head. Center the 2-pound ball of clay.

2 Open the clay until it's about $4\frac{1}{2}$″ to 5″ inches across. Be sure to open the clay with a flat center, and not a curved base like in the cup. To ensure a flat base, keep your fingers horizontal to the wheel head as you draw them outward. The base should be flat from center to about 2″ out from center (photo A). The thickness of the base should be about $\frac{1}{2}$″ to accommodate the foot that will be trimmed later.

3 When the base is the right diameter, open the clay to form a shallow, curved saucer. Move the clay outward until the saucer measures $8\frac{1}{2}$″ from rim to rim.

4 As you open the clay, be sure to stretch it slightly upward as you pull outward. Start each movement at the center of the form, continually supporting underneath the clay with your outside finger-tips as you work (photo B). Working slowly and methodically with a slow wheel speed is best; as the saucer gets wider, decrease the wheel speed.

5 Use a damp sponge to clean up the base and to remove any slip from the underside of the saucer. With the tip of a wooden rib, cut a groove at the base of the saucer.

6 Next, you'll create the well in the center of the saucer. This well keeps the foot of the cup securely in place and centered in the saucer. Use the rounded corner of a wooden rib to define the outside perimeter of the well (photo C). Lightly press the flat end of the rib, with the rounded corner facing out, into the center of the saucer.

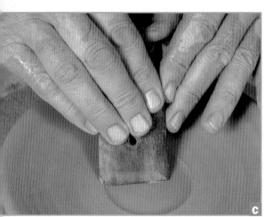

7 Measure the diameter of the slight depression with a ruler. The well should be $2\frac{1}{2}$″ across. When the diameter is right, press firmly into the saucer with the end of the rib to create a deeper well. The step down from the slope of the saucer to the bottom, or floor, of the well should be about $\frac{1}{8}$″. Smooth the interior of the saucer, then remove any slip in the well with a damp sponge.

8 Create a groove just inside the rim of the saucer with the sharp tip of a wooden rib. This groove, or step, makes the saucer easier to pick up and hold. It also completes the form aesthetically, giving a finished edge to the saucer. Be sure to support the saucer underneath the rim with your left hand as you push the rib into the clay (photo D).

9 Stop the wheel, then pull a cut-off wire under the saucer to release it from the bat. The groove cut into the base will guide the wire as it slides flat and straight beneath the saucer. Remove the bat from the wheel head with your saucer attached.

THROWING THE HANDLE

1 The handle of the cup is thrown "off the hump." To form the hump, center a 1-pound ball of clay in a cone shape directly on the wheel head. The centered hump will be about 3″ in diameter at the base, 2″ in diameter at the top, and 3″ tall. Open the clay hump to a depth of about 1″ to form a short, thick cylinder at the top of the hump.

2 Pull the thick cylinder upward until it's 2½″ tall, using plenty of water to make the pulls. As the clay stretches and the cylinder narrows, use an index and middle finger on the outside and an index finger inside the cylinder to pull.

3 The wall should be a little less than ¼″ thick. If the wall is too thick, the extra weight of the handle could pull the cup out of shape when it's fired.

4 Begin to shape the handle. The tapered handle should be shaped to fit your hand: wider in the middle and narrower at each end. Taper the cylinder by gently compressing the clay between your two thumbs and index fingers. Place your fingers and thumbs just above the solid base at the bottom of the cylinder (photo A), then relax and glide your fingertips up the form.

5 Near the top of the cylinder, taper in again by gently compressing the clay inward. Round the top of the cylinder, but don't close it completely. Leave a hole about ⅛″ in diameter at the very top (photo B).

6 With a soft rubber rib, remove the slip from the outside of the handle and smooth the surface. Then cut a circular groove at the base of the handle with the tip of a wooden rib or an undercutting rib.

7 Adjust the wheel to a slow speed. Place a cut-off wire into the groove, and then quickly pull it through the clay. Dry your fingertips, pick up the handle, and place it on a clean, dry surface.

8 The entire length of the handle should be hollow. Once the handle is attached to the cup, one end will be sealed. The hole in the other end allows the air to escape so the handle won't explode in the kiln when it shrinks during firing. Set the cup, saucer, and handle aside to air-dry until they are leather hard.

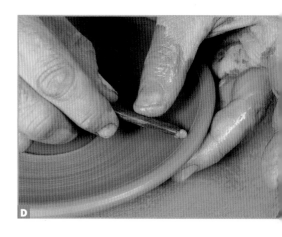

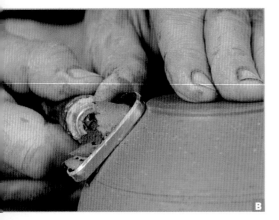

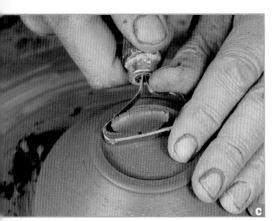

▚ TRIMMING ▚

1 To trim the base of the cup and the saucer, throw a clay trimming pad on the wheel head. (To make a clay trimming pad, see page 38, step 2.) The pad should be 9˝ in diameter, or a bit larger than the diameter of the saucer.

2 To trim the cup, invert it on the trimming pad. Center the cup, then press down on it gently to ensure a strong attachment. With a looped trimming tool and a quick wheel speed, remove the excess clay from the base. Smooth the side of the cup with the straight blade of the tool for a graceful curve (photo A).

3 Next, define the foot of the cup. The outside diameter of the foot is going to be 2¼˝ across, because it must fit easily inside the well of the saucer, which is 2½˝ across. Measure the base, then mark the outside diameter of the foot. With the wide end of the trimming tool, make an indent at the outside edge of the foot, which gives the foot a ¼˝ rise (photo B). Now measure in ¼˝ from the outside edge of the foot and make an indent to mark the inside edge of the foot.

4 With the narrow end of the tool, remove the clay from the base inside the foot ring. The base should be about ¼˝ thick, or the same thickness as the wall (photo C). Smooth the foot ring with your fingertips (photo D).

5 Dampen the wall with a sponge, then burnish the side of the cup with a soft rubber rib. When finished, gently grasp the cup at each side and release it from the pad, setting it on a clean wareboard.

6 Next, trim the saucer. Before trimming, make sure the saucer is stiff-leather hard so it won't warp when you trim it or pick it up off the clay pad.

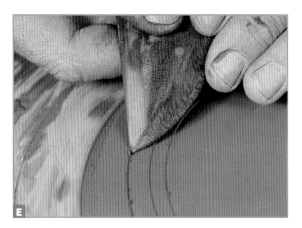

7 Use a stiff rib to smooth and level the clay trimming pad. Mark a few concentric circles on the pad with the sharp tip of a wooden rib or with your fingernail. These rings are guides to centering the saucer on the pad for trimming (photo E).

8 Cut a keyhole at the edge of the clay pad with the tip of your thumb. This will allow you to slip your finger under the trimmed saucer and pop it loose from the pad (photo F).

9 Center the saucer upside down on the clay pad, then press it down gently to ensure a strong attachment. Use a quick wheel speed and the trimming tool to remove the excess clay from the bottom of the saucer. The foot should be about half the diameter of the saucer, or about 4½″ across.

10 Measure the outside diameter of the foot and mark it. Move in ¼″ and mark the inside diameter. With the trimming tool, define the outside stepped edge. Like the foot of the cup, there should be a rise of about ¼″.

11 Trim the excess clay inside the foot ring. Using the tool at the 3 o'clock position on the wheel head, trim from the center out to the foot ring (photo G). Make sure enough clay has been removed so the saucer won't "sit" on its center. To check this, lay a ruler across the bottom of the saucer. The ruler should only touch the foot ring, not the base (photo H).

12 Smooth the foot ring and the bottom of the saucer inside the foot ring with your fingertip. Dampen the rest of the trimmed surface with a sponge, then burnish it with a soft rubber rib. When finished, use the keyhole to pop the saucer off the trimming pad. Set the saucer aside.

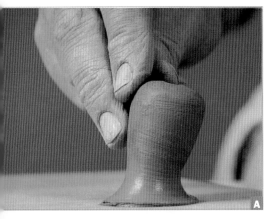

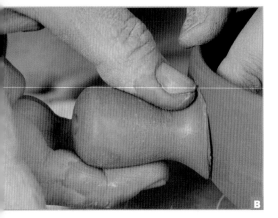

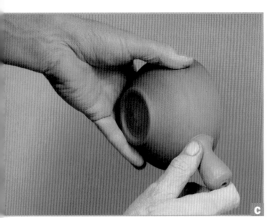

ATTACHING THE HANDLE

1 Now you'll attach the handle to the cup. Dip the wire-cut end of the handle in water, then place the handle upright on a clean wareboard. When the base is soft, tilt the handle to one side; an angle of about 70° is good. This makes the cup easy to pick up without bumping your fingers against the saucer (photo A).

2 Wet the end of the handle again with a wet fingertip or sponge. Carefully place the wet end of the handle onto the side of the cup about ⅛″ below the rim. The handle should tilt upward as you secure it to the cup. Support the cup inside with your fingertips while you press the handle tightly to the outside (photo B).

3 Wet your thumb and press around the outside edge of the handle to seal the edge against the cup (photo C). Use a wet sponge to smooth the joint; don't try to eliminate the seam, just soften it.

4 Adjust the handle so it has a definite upward tilt toward the rim of the cup. When finished, sign or add your signature stamp to the base area. Set the cup and saucer aside to air-dry until they are bone dry.

FIRING, WAXING, & GLAZING

1 Carefully place the pieces into the kiln for the first firing. Fire the bisque kiln to approximately 1750° Fahrenheit for about 10 to 12 hours. When the bisque kiln has cooled to 200° Fahrenheit or less, it's ready to open.

2 Before glazing the soup cup and saucer, apply wax-resist emulsion to the base of each piece.

3 For an even wax line, rotate the pieces on a banding wheel while applying the wax emulsion with a narrow foam brush. Make sure to wax the foot of the cup, inside the cup's foot ring (photo A), the foot of the saucer, a small circle inside the saucer's foot ring (photo B), and the well. If the clay in the well is bare, the pieces can be fired together. Also, when in use, the cup won't slide around on the saucer if the well has been waxed. Set the pieces aside until the wax emulsion is dry to the touch.

4 To glaze the soup cup and saucer, select two contrasting but compatible glazes. Stir up the first glaze; this is the base glaze, and it will be used on the inside and outside of the cup and saucer.

5 Dip the cup and then the saucer into the first glaze, holding on to the waxed areas where possible. Keep each piece submerged for about three seconds. Place the pieces on a clean wareboard, then immediately touch up any areas of bare clay with a dab of glaze (photo C). When the sheen has gone off the pots, the first layer of glaze is dry.

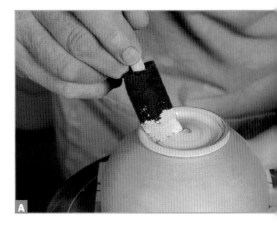
A

B

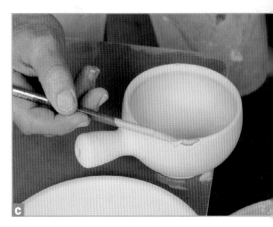
C

TIPS | DIY Network Crafts

To add visual interest to the coiled handles, cut two squares of old car mat, doormat, or any kind of rubber mat with a textured surfaces. Roll the clay coil between the two mats to texture the clay. Experiment! Try rolling the mats over the coils multiple times and in several directions for unique and exciting textures.

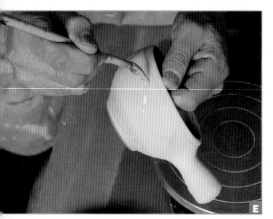

6 Clean the waxed base areas with a damp sponge to remove any excess glaze beads that might have adhered to the waxed surfaces.

7 Place the cup upside down on the banding wheel. With a small foam brush, wax over the first layer of glaze about one-third of the way up the side of the cup. Using a fine-tipped brush, add a thin line of wax just below the larger waxed area (photo D).

8 Turn the cup upright and wax another line around and just below the rim. Another thin line is fine — just enough to define the top of the cup is needed.

9 With a fine-tipped brush and wax-resist emulsion, paint on the area that is not already waxed to add a design to the side of the cup. Do any pattern you like; in this set, I've quickly stroked a series of Xs using a Japanese paintbrush (photo E). Set the cup aside to dry when finished.

10 Stir up the second glaze. Spread your hand inside the cup to hold it steady, then dip the outside of the cup, base first, up to the rim. Keep the cup as level as possible so glaze doesn't flow inside. Keep the cup submerged for two seconds or less (photo F).

Soup Cup & Saucer Glaze Recipe

The primary glaze is Raspberry Red. It's a glossy glaze fired to cone 6 in oxidation. The secondary glaze, Nutmeg, is opaque semi-matte and also fired to cone 6 in oxidation.

RASPBERRY RED:		NUTMEG:	
Nepheline Syenite	18.0%	Dolomite	23.3%
Ferro Frit #3134	14.0%	Spodumene (Australian)	23.3%
Whiting	20.0%	OM #4 Ball Clay	23.3%
OM-4 Ball Clay	18.0%	Silica	23.3%
Silica	30.0%	Ferro Frit #3134	6.8%
	100%		100.0%
ADD:		**ADD:**	
Chrome Oxide	0.20%	Red Iron Oxide	1.07%
Tin Oxide	3.75%	Yellow Ochre	3.24%
		Tin Oxide	4.85%
		Bentonite	1.90%

11 Place the saucer on the banding wheel right side up. With a foam brush, apply wax onto the rim. Then apply a band of wax that covers the well and about ½″ beyond the edge of the well.

12 Dip the saucer into the second glaze. Sponge the cup and saucer to remove any glaze beads from the waxed areas. When the cup and saucer are dry, place them into the kiln for the second firing. Fire the cup on the saucer to save kiln space. The kiln should fire to cone 6, or about 2200° Fahrenheit, for about 10 to 12 hours. Let the kiln cool for an additional 36 hours before unloading it.

HANDBUILT HANDLE

The soup cup takes on an entirely different look with a handbuilt handle. Just as functional, and a lot easier to make, this style of handle gives a more creative, whimsical look to the cup and saucer set. Try them both to see which one suits you best.

1 Roll out a tapered coil of clay between 5″ and 6″ long. It should measure ¾″ at the widest end, and ¼″ at the other end. Add texture to the coil for interest (photo A).

2 Wet the wide end of the coil with water. Attach the wide end of the coil to the cup about 1″ above the foot, pressing firmly. Now wet the area just below the rim with water where the other end of the coil will be attached to the cup. Bend the coil up to the rim, then press the end gently to the cup, supporting the inside with your fingertips.

3 Use a small diameter wooden dowel to secure the top end of the coiled handle to the cup. Support the inside of the cup opposite the handle as you press firmly with the dowel (photo B). Push the handle upward slightly to give it the right lift (photo C).

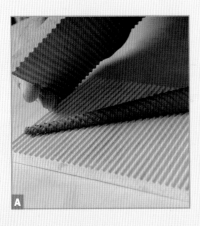

A

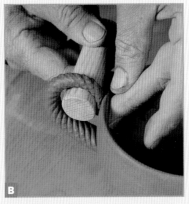

B

C

DINNER PLATES

Many exciting projects can be mastered once you've acquired the skills to make a low, wide form. For this project, I've made three sizes of plates to create a place setting with a bread and butter plate, a salad plate, and a dinner plate. Two design elements — a wide rim and a glazing technique — unify the set.

◢◤ PROJECT SUMMARY ◥◣

The key to making matching pieces like this set is repetition. I've thrown and trimmed a uniform group of plates by repeating the same movements in the same order using the same tools. To finish the set, I've glazed the plates with a simple cross-dipping technique. If you practice perfecting your skills with this project, you'll soon have a cabinet full of terrific tableware to share with family and guests.

You Will Need

Materials:

- 9½ pounds of very soft clay (for the plates)
- 3 pounds of clay (for the trimming pad)
- Small ball of clay (for the pointer)
- Wax-resist emulsion
- Two glazes
- Bucket of water

Tools:

- 3 bats (2 medium and 1 large)
- Banding wheel
- Small sponge
- Soft rubber rib
- Large soft rubber rib
- Stiff rubber rib
- Undercutting stick
- Needle tool
- Looped trimming tool
- Pointer or chopstick
- Ruler
- Cut-off wire
- Dishpan or wide bucket
- Narrow foam brush
- Signature stamp (optional)

THROWING THE SMALL PLATE

1 To make this three-piece place setting on the potter's wheel, weigh out 9½ pounds of very soft clay. The softer the clay, the easier it will be to pull each flat form outward.

2 Divide the clay into three lumps: 4½ pounds for the largest plate, 3½ pounds for the medium plate, and 1½ pounds for the small plate. Knead each lump thoroughly to remove air pockets.

3 Attach a bat to the wheel head. Since it's almost impossible to remove a low, wide form from the wheel without severely distorting it, plates should always be thrown on a bat.

4 Begin with the smallest plate, using the 1½-pound ball of clay. While making the first plate, you'll establish the order, tools, and techniques for making the larger plates.

5 To begin, center the clay and then open it, keeping your fingertips horizontal to the wheel head as you draw them outward.

6 The base of each small plate should be ½″ thick and 6″ in diameter. In order to trim a raised foot later, it's essential to leave enough clay at the base now. Use the needle tool to measure the thickness of the base. (See page 34, step 8 for directions on using a needle tool.)

7 Although the plates appear flat when finished, they're actually thrown in a very shallow, bowl-shaped curve. As the plates dry and the clay shrinks, the center will rise up to create a convex dome shape. To compensate for this natural distortion, plates should be thrown with a curved inside floor so the center becomes flat as the clay dries and shrinks.

8 To draw the clay outward, start each movement at the center of the form. Pull and press the clay outward toward the 5 o'clock position on the wheel head.

9 When the base measures 3″ in diameter, relax the downward pressure as your fingertips near the outer edge. This creates the shallow curve in the floor of the plate.

10 Support the outer edge of the clay with your thumb and outside fingertips as you work. Supporting the outside edge keeps the clay from opening and spreading wider than needed (photo A). Decrease the wheel speed as the plate gets wider; working with a slow to medium wheel speed is best for low, wide forms.

11 Before shaping the rim, measure the diameter of the plate to make sure it's about 7″ across, including the unfinished rim. To form the rim, sandwich the clay between the fingertips of both hands. One hand should be positioned inside the plate while the other hand's fingertips are placed beneath the thick rim (photo B).

12 Now press up from beneath the rim, pushing the clay into the fingertips of your inside hand. The groove between the index and middle fingers of the inside hand creates a step that separates the rim from the floor of the plate. Once this inner step is formed, lightly pull the clay outward to form a tapered rim. The rim should be angled slightly upward, not flat or parallel to the wheel head (photo C).

13 Remove the water from inside the plate with a sponge, then smooth the inside of the plate with a soft rubber rib. Placing the rib between the 11 and 12 o'clock position on the plate allows you to see exactly what the rib is doing on the surface of the plate (photo D).

14 Next, smooth the rim using the rib in the 5 o'clock position on the plate. Support beneath the rim with your outside fingertips as you press the rib onto the rim (photo E). Soften and clean up the edges and rim of the plate with a sponge.

15 Create a swirl by sliding your thumb tip into the center of the plate in one quick motion, starting the slide about 1″ from center. This swirl adds visual interest and movement to the finished piece.

16 With the beveled end of an undercutting stick, cut a small bevel beneath the plate at the base.

17 Now stop the wheel. Pull a cut-off wire under the plate to free it from the bat, keeping the wire as taught as possible between your fingertips so it cuts flat and straight beneath the plate. Pull the wire toward you, from 12 o'clock to 6 o'clock.

18 Remove the bat from the wheel head with the plate attached. Set the plate aside to air-dry until very stiff-leather hard.

19 Trim, wax, glaze, and fire the plates as the following instructions direct.

TIPS | DIY Network Crafts

To make multiple plates of the same size, use the same weight of clay for each plate.

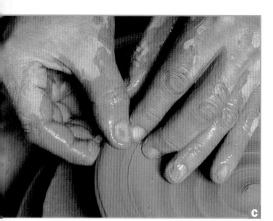

◀▦ THROWING THE MEDIUM PLATE ▦▶

1 Except for the amount of clay you work with, throwing a medium-sized plate is very similar to throwing a small one. First, attach another bat to the wheel head and use the 3½-pound lump of clay. This salad plate will be 10˝ in diameter when wet, including the rim.

2 Center the clay and open it, keeping your fingers horizontal to the wheel head as you draw them outward. Leave the base ½˝ thick to accommodate the trimmed foot.

3 Relax your fingertip pressure slightly as you move toward the edge of the form. Like on the smaller plate, this will create the very shallow, curved interior floor. Compress the inside surface by running your fingertips from the center to the edge and back several times. Support and contain the edge of the clay as you work.

4 Next, draw the clay outward to finish forming the plate. As you stretch the clay outward from the center, keep the form convex; remember, you don't want to throw the plate flat. Support the edge of the clay with your outside fingertips (photo A) and decrease the wheel speed as the plate gets wider.

5 When the clay is opened to about 8˝, begin to form the rim. The rim should be angled slightly upward toward the outer edge, not parallel to the wheel head.

6 To form the rim, sandwich the clay between your fingertips. Place one hand inside the plate and the other hand beneath the thick rim. Push up with the fingertips beneath the rim, pressing the clay into the groove between the index and middle fingers of the top hand (photo B). This creates the step that separates the rim from the floor of the plate, which should be ½˝ deep. Once the inner step is established, gently pull the clay outward to form the tapered rim (photo C).

7 Remove the excess water from inside the plate with a sponge. Smooth the inside of the plate and the rim with a soft rubber rib, then use a sponge to soften the rim edges.

8 Next, create the decorative swirl in the center of the plate. When finished, cut a bevel at the base of the plate with the beveled end of an undercutting stick.

9 Separate the plate from the bat with a cut-off wire. Remove the bat from the wheel head with the plate still attached, then set it aside until the plate dries to very stiff-leather hard.

10 Trim, wax, glaze, and fire the plates as the following instructions direct.

THROWING THE LARGE PLATE

1 Except for the amount of clay you work with, throwing a large-sized plate is very similar to throwing a medium-sized one. The wet plate will be 11½″ in diameter when finished.

2 To start, center the 4½-pound lump of very soft clay and then open it, leaving the base ½″ thick to accommodate the trimmed foot.

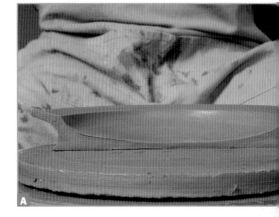

3 Draw the clay outward to form the slightly curved inside floor of the plate (photo A). Compress the inside surface, supporting beneath the outer edge of the clay with your outside fingers and thumb tips (photo B). Decrease the wheel speed as the diameter increases.

4 Form the rim when the inside floor of the plate is 9½″ in diameter. At about 1¼″ across, this rim will be a little wider than those on the other two plates. All proportions should increase in scale as you increase the size of the plate.

5 To form the rim, sandwich the clay between your fingertips, placing one hand inside the plate with the fingertips of the other hand placed beneath the thick outer edge. Push upward with the fingertips from beneath the rim, pressing the clay into the groove between the index and middle fingers of the top hand to create a step (photo C). This step down separates the rim from the inside floor of the plate; it should measure a bit more than ½″ tall.

6 Once the inner step is established, gently pull the clay outward to form the tapered rim (photo D, following page). Support below the rim with your fingertips as you work. Remove the excess water from inside the plate with a sponge. Then use a large, soft rubber rib to smooth the rim and the inside surface of the plate.

7 Next, create the swirl in the center. On this plate, make the diameter of the swirl bigger in proportion to the larger plate (photo E). When finished, cut a bevel at the base of the plate with the beveled end of an undercutting stick.

8 With the tip of your finger, press down on the rim very lightly to adjust its slope. This should be a subtle movement providing a final, gentle adjustment.

9 Now separate the plate from the bat with a cut-off wire. Remove the bat from the wheel head with the plate attached, then set it aside until the plate dries to very stiff-leather hard.

10 Trim, wax, glaze, and fire the plates as the following instructions direct.

TIPS | DIY Network Crafts

To make multiple plates that all look alike, use the same tools in the same order with the same motions on every plate.

TRIMMING ALL PLATE SIZES

1 To trim the plates, throw a large clay trimming pad with a 3-pound lump of clay. First, center the clay directly on the wheel head, then open the clay until the diameter is at least 1″ larger than the biggest plate. Be sure the surface of the pad is level before moving ahead.

2 Skim the surface of the pad with a stiff rib to remove the slip and excess water. With the tip of a wooden rib, mark several concentric circles in the pad to assist in centering the plates on the pad (photo A). Use the tip of your thumb or a looped trimming tool to cut a keyhole at the edge of the pad. You'll use this later to remove the plate from the pad when finished trimming (photo B).

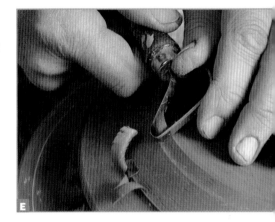

3 Center the largest plate upside down on the pad. Secure the plate to the pad by pressing down on the edge of the rim with a fingertip as the wheel slowly rotates.

4 With the straight blade of the looped trimming tool, remove the excess clay from the outside base area of the plate (photo C). As you trim the plate, keep in mind that the interior shape of the plate should be mirrored on the underside. The goal is to have an even ¼˝ thickness throughout the plate.

5 Where the inside edge of the rim steps down into the surface of the plate, trim a step on the underside of the plate. To do this, use the straight blade of the trimming tool on the underside of the rim to trim a flat surface equal to the rim's width. With the narrow end of the tool, trim a small step to separate the rim from the rest of the trimmed plate (photo D).

6 With the straight blade of the tool, trim the sloping underside of the plate. This surface should correspond to the sloped area inside the plate where the step drops down from the rim to the floor.

7 Next, trim the raised foot. Begin by creating a waxing guideline at the outside edge of the flat base. At the same time, define the outside shape of the foot ring (photo E).

8 To create the inside edge of the foot ring, measure in ¼˝ from the outside edge of the foot and mark it with your fingernail. Use the straight blade of the trimming tool to remove ¼˝ of clay from the base inside the foot ring. As you work, move the tool from the center out to the rim of the foot. Neaten the interior wall of the foot ring with the narrow end of the tool (photo F, following page), and then smooth it with a fingertip.

9 With a damp sponge, smooth over the trimmed surfaces. If the clay you're using contains an aggregate, use a soft rubber rib to burnish the trimmed surfaces (photo G).

10 Sign the plate near the foot ring or stamp it with your "chop" (a potter's signature seal). Release the plate from the trimming pad using the keyhole. Set the plate aside on a clean, dry surface, then check the rim to make sure no clay has adhered to it from the trimming pad.

11 Now center the medium-sized plate on the trimming pad. Follow the same steps to trim the medium and small plates as you did to trim the largest plate. Here are the basic steps again:

12 Remove the excess clay from the base where the plate was attached to the bat, then trim the underside of the rim. Trim a step to mirror the interior step, and then trim the sloping side of the plate to mirror the interior curve. Trim a waxing guideline and establish the outside edge of the foot ring.

13 Establish the inside edge of the foot ring. Trim the excess clay from inside the foot ring until the plate is ¼″ thick, then smooth the ring with your fingertip. Smooth the trimmed surfaces with a damp sponge, burnishing the surface if necessary.

14 Sign the plate or use your signature stamp, then release the plate from the trimming pad. Check for pieces of clay that might have adhered to the rim, then place the trimmed plate on a clean surface.

TIPS | DIY Network Crafts

To make multiple plates of exactly the same height and diameter, attach a marker, or pointer, to the edge of the wheel tray with a ball of clay. Use a pointed chopstick or similar object to make the pointer. After throwing the first plate, place the pointer at the rim. Then throw each successive plate until the edge of the rim extends to the tip of the pointer.

◢◢◢ FIRING, WAXING, & GLAZING ◢◢◢

1 When all of the plates have air-dried completely, load them into the kiln for their first firing. You can stack the plates, one on top of the other, with refractory spacers placed between each plate. Use the spacers in an in-line, tripod configuration (photo A).

2 Fire the bisque kiln to approximately 1750° Fahrenheit for about 10 to 12 hours. When the bisque kiln has cooled to 200° Fahrenheit or less, it's ready to open.

3 For an even wax line, rotate the plates on a banding wheel while applying the wax emulsion with a narrow foam brush. Elevating the plates on a piece of pottery to apply the wax helps keep their rims clean of any wax that might adhere to the surface of the banding wheel (photo B).

4 Apply wax-resist emulsion to the foot rings of each plate and on the sides following the wax guideline. Be sure to wax the inside corner of the foot ring (photo C).

5 It's a good idea to also wax a small circular area in the center of each plate so it won't accidentally fuse to the kiln shelf during the glaze firing (photo D, page 83). Let the wax dry for about 10 minutes, or until it is dry to the touch.

6 To glaze the plates, select two complementary glaze colors. Stir up the first glaze, then pour it into a dishpan or a wide, low bucket. The bucket must be large enough to comfortably fit the largest plate with some room to spare.

7 Hold the largest plate at one side. Dip three-quarters of the plate into the glaze, wiggling it left and right to create an interesting wavy line at the top of the dip (photo E, page 83).

8 Let the plate drip dry over the glaze bucket. This prevents unwanted drips and streaks of glaze from running across the surface of the plate.

9 Set the plate aside on a clean surface to air-dry. Dip the medium and small plates the same way, wiggling them to create the wavy edge across the top of the plate. When the plates are dry, use a damp sponge to clean the waxed areas.

10 Stir up the second glaze thoroughly to get all of the glaze particles into suspension. Pour the glaze into another clean dishpan or a wide, low bucket.

A

B

C

RIM EMBELLISHING OPTIONS

Add some sophistication to your handmade plates by using a simple wiggle-wire to create a variety of unique rim surfaces. Decide if you want to decorate the rims before you throw; the rim of these plates will need to be thicker than normal —½″ thick — to use the wiggle-wire.

1 To account for the thicker rim, add 6 ounces of clay to each lump when you throw the small and medium sized plates. 8 extra ounces of clay should be added to each lump for a thicker rim on the large plates.

2 To decorate the rim, hold the wire tightly between the fingertips of each hand. Position the wire over the plate at 3 o'clock on the wheel head (photo A).

3 As the plate slowly turns, quickly lower the wire into the rim about ¼″ deep. The wire should remain buried in the rim during one revolution of the wheel.

4 As soon as the wire is imbedded in the clay rim, wiggle the wire. Keep the wire horizontal within the rim as you wiggle it.

5 For a uniform pattern, maintain a repetitive rhythmic motion. You can also mix it up a bit by holding the wire still, then wiggling it, then holding it still, and so on. There are numerous possibilities, so experiment and have fun (photos B, C, and D).

6 When you've reached the wire's starting point after one revolution, quickly pull it up and out of the rim.

7 Stop the wheel, and then use the tip of a needle tool to carefully lift off the top section of the rim that was cut away. Use a damp sponge to soften the inner and outer edges of the rim.

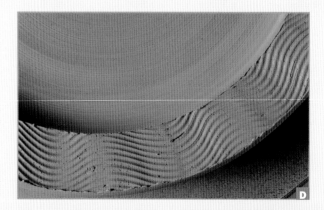

11 Starting with the largest plate, dip the bare clay edge into the glaze, overlapping the glazes at least an inch or two. Wiggle the plate left and right to create a second wavy line where the glaze coats overlap (photo F).

12 Let the plate drip over the glaze bucket again, then set it aside to air-dry. Use a damp sponge to clean the excess glaze from the waxed areas of each plate.

13 Place the plates in the kiln for the final firing. The kiln should fire to cone 6, or about 2200° Fahrenheit, for about 10 to 12 hours. Let the kiln cool for an additional 36 hours before unloading it.

14 Now enjoy using your handmade plates. They'll clean up easily in the dishwasher, and they're also microwave and oven safe.

D

E

F

Plates Glaze Recipe

The primary glaze is Cream Rust. The secondary glaze is Nutmeg, which is an opaque semi-matte glaze. Both glazes are fired to cone 6 in oxidation.

CREAM RUST:

Custer Feldspar	26.6%
Strontium Carbonate	3.3%
Ferro Frit #3134	30.6%
Wollastonite	10.6%
Talc	2.3%
EPK	8.4%
Silica	18.2%
	100.0%

ADD:

Red Iron Oxide	6.00%
Tin Oxide	13.00

NUTMEG:

Domite	23.3%
Spodumene (Australian)	23.3%
OM #4 Ball Clay	23.3%
Silica	23.3%
Ferro Frit #3134	6.8%
	100.0%

ADD:

Red Iron Oxide	1.07%
Yellow Ochre	3.24%
Tin Oxide	4.85%
Bentonite	1.90%

BUTTER DISH

This covered butter dish is both attractive and versatile. I use it to store cream cheese, hard cheese, and other spreads in addition to butter and margarine.

◀◀ PROJECT SUMMARY ▶▶

I created this covered butter dish by throwing two shallow bowls on the potter's wheel. One shallow bowl becomes the lid, to which I add a knob. I enjoy making different kinds of knobs to top off this great project, as each style gives the covered dish a unique look. The other shallow bowl becomes the base of the dish. I split the rim of this bowl to create a sturdy neck that holds the lid in place on the base. Splitting the rim also forms a wide ledge that makes the dish easy to pick up.

You Will Need

Materials:

- 3 pounds 4 ounces of stoneware clay
- 8 ounces of very soft clay
- Wax-resist emulsion
- Two complementary glazes

Tools:

- Two small bats and a pair of bat pins
- Banding wheel
- Ruler or measuring calipers
- Undercutting rib
- Soft rubber rib
- Looped trimming tool
- Tapered hole cutter
- Cut-off wire
- Small sponge
- Narrow foam brush
- Small pointed brush
- Signature stamp (optional)

THROWING THE BASE

1 To prepare for throwing at the potter's wheel, weigh out three balls of stoneware clay: one 1¼ pounds and two weighing 1 pound each. Knead the balls thoroughly to remove air pockets and homogenize the clay.

2 Place a bat on the wheel head. Throwing the base and lid of the covered dish on bats ensures that the wet clay forms can be transferred from the wheel head to the drying rack without being distorted.

3 To throw the base of the covered dish, first center the 1¼-pound ball of clay on the bat. Use enough water to wet the clay so it slides easily beneath your fingers and palms.

A

B

4 The next step is to open the clay. Press the index and middle finger of one hand and the thumb of your other hand into the center of the ball (photo A, previous page). Draw your hands outward, leaving a little more than 1/4˝ of clay between the wheel head and your fingertips; this distance is the thickness of the dish's base. As you draw your fingers outward, keep them horizontal to the wheel head (photo B, previous page). This position ensures a flat base on the bottom of the dish.

5 With all the fingers of one hand, move back and forth several times from the center to the outside wall of clay, keeping your hands parallel to the wheel head. This action compresses the clay and ensures that the base of the dish will dry flat.

6 The next step is to make the first pull on the wall of the bowl. Pulling the wall and drawing the clay upward takes several hand positions.

7 First, tuck a thumb under the outside of the form at the base of the wall. Then force your thumb under the clay to push a groove into the base of the wall (photo C). Tuck your middle and ring fingers into the groove at the base of the wall, then slide the clay upward from the base to the rim. Keep your other hand inside the pot, opposite the outside fingertips, as you pull the clay upward (photo D).

8 The rim should be thick. As you reach the top of the pot with each pull, capture the clay between your fingertips. Keep your thumb pressed across the top of the rim, compressing the clay slightly. This action limits the rise of the wall and ensures a thick rim (photo E).

9 When the wall is about 1½˝ tall, split the rim. This forms the outside ledge (where the lid will sit) and also the neck (which will hold the lid in place on the dish's base). Splitting the rim is a multi-step-process. First, place your fin-

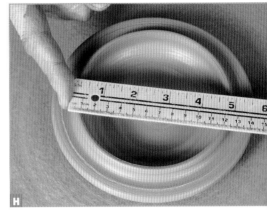

gers underneath the outside of the rim (photo F). Then place your thumb in the middle of the rim, dividing it in half. Push down with your thumb on the outside half of the rim; this pressure separates the rim, dividing it to make the ledge and the neck of the dish (photo G).

10 To form the ledge, squeeze the depressed clay between your fingers and stretch it outward. The outside diameter of this ledge should measure 6¼″. The remaining clay is the neck of the dish, and its outside diameter should measure 5″ (photo H).

11 To define the angle between the neck and the ledge, use an undercutting rib. Place the short angle of the rib into the corner and press downward. As you do this, support underneath the outside ledge with your fingertips (photo I). Stretch the neck upward slightly to further define the split rim.

12 Measure the outside diameter of the ledge and the neck again, adjusting until the dimensions are exact. If the overall diameter is too small, capture the ledge and neck with your fingertips and gently stretch the clay outward at the 3 o'clock position on the wheel head. If the overall diameter is too big, capture all of the parts and gently coax the clay inward. Adjust in very small increments and measure often.

13 Remove the excess water from the inside and outside of the form with a damp sponge.

14 To add visual movement to the finished piece, make a swirl in the base of the dish. Use a fingertip or the side of your thumb and, with a slight downward pressure, slide it from outside to center with one quick motion (photo J).

15 With a cut-off wire, cut the dish loose from the bat, then set it aside. Let the base of the butter dish air-dry until it's leather hard.

◄◄ THROWING THE LID ►►

1 To throw the lid of the butter dish, place another small bat on the wheel head. Center a 1-pound ball of clay on the bat.

2 Now open the clay. Press the index and middle finger of one hand and the thumb of your other hand into the center of the ball; press downward, then draw your hands outward. Leave ¼″ of clay between the wheel head and your fingertips to form the thickness of the lid. As you open the clay, form a shallow curve in the base by relaxing your fingers as you draw them outward (photo A).

3 Pull the wall to form the depth of the lid. Drawing the clay upward takes several hand positions. First, tuck a thumb under the base of the form, then force it under the clay to push a groove at the base of the wall. Tuck your index, middle, and ring fingers into the groove, then slide the clay from the base to the rim. Keep your other hand inside the lid, opposite the outside hand, to coax the clay to the rim.

4 As you make the lid, keep the wall vertical initially. Then, to give the lid its domed shape, gently flare the wall by stretching it slightly outward (photo B).

5 Keep the rim thick and strong, but not heavy like the rim on the bottom of the butter dish. The rim should be rounded and a little less than ¼″ thick.

6 When the wall is about 1″ tall, measure the inside diameter of the lid. It should be 5⅛″, or slightly larger than the diameter of the base's neck. If the diameter is too small, gently coax the form outward with your fingers at the 3 o'clock position on the wheel head. Adjust the angle of the wall as you stretch the lid outward.

7 If the diameter is too big, gently coax the clay inward by placing the palms of both hands flat against the clay at the 12 o'clock position on the wheel head; gently press inward. Again, resize the shape of the lid as you adjust the diameter.

8 Clean up the inside and outside of the form with a damp sponge, removing excess water and finger marks. Cut the lid from the bat with a cut-off wire.

9 Remove the bat from the wheel head and set it aside. Let the lid air-dry until it's leather hard.

TRIMMING

1 To trim the base and the lid of the butter dish, make a clay trimming pad with the remaining 1-pound ball of soft clay. The tacky clay surface holds the pieces firmly to the wheel head as you trim.

2 To make a clay trimming pad, center the clay directly on the wheel head. Open the clay until the diameter is at least as large as the base of the butter dish, taking care to make sure the surface is level. Skim the surface with a rubber rib, removing the slip and excess water. With the tip of your finger or a wooden rib, mark several concentric circles in the pad. These circles are guidelines that assist in centering the pot on the pad (photo A).

3 Cut a keyhole at the edge of the clay pad. This will let you slip your finger under the pot and pop it loose from the pad when finished trimming (photo B).

4 To trim the base, invert it on the trimming pad. Center the base on the pad, then press down on it gently to ensure a strong attachment. With a looped trimming tool and a quick wheel speed, carve away the excess clay from the base until it's a little less than ¼″ thick. Mirror the interior shape of the dish to ensure an even thickness and an aesthetically pleasing shape. Specifically, where the outside rim, or ledge, is flat on the topside of the dish, trim a flat area on the underside of the dish (photo C). Then trim a sloped bevel from the floor area to the foot. (photo D).

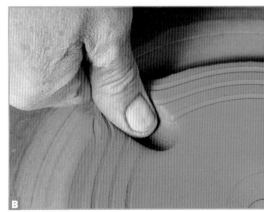

5 With the side of your fingernail, press into the clay to frame the textured base pattern (photo E). Then dampen the trimmed area with a damp sponge. Burnish the trimmed surface smooth with a soft rubber rib or the tip of your finger. When finished, sign the underside of the butter dish or use your signature stamp somewhere on or near the base (photo F).

6 Using the keyhole, release the base from the pad (photo G), then check the rim to make sure clay from the pad isn't stuck to it. If there is clay on the rim, wipe it clean with a damp sponge or your fingertips. Set the base aside to air-dry until bone dry.

7 To trim the lid, place it right side up on the trimming pad (photo H). Center the lid and press it gently to the clay pad. With the long side of the blade of a looped trimming tool, remove the excess clay to give the top of the lid a domed shape. Again, the exterior shape of the lid should mirror the interior shape (photo I).

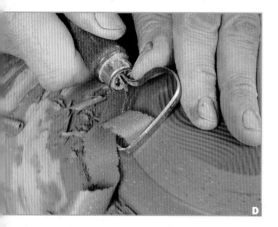

8 As you trim the lid, don't remove clay from the rim. The rim should stay thick and strong to prevent it from chipping when in use. After trimming the basic shape, test the lid for uniform thickness. With your fingertips on the inside and outside of the lid, feel the cross section; it should be a little less than ¼″ thick (photo J).

9 Center the lid on the trimming pad again and press it tightly to ensure a good seal. Now you're ready to attach a knob.

ATTACHING A KNOB

1 Now it's time to attach a thrown knob on top of the lid. There are several kinds of knobs you can use on this project — see the sidebar on pages 96 and 97 for more ideas.

2 Attaching a thrown knob is basically like throwing a small pot on top of the lid. First, with the wheel slowly spinning, score the top of the lid with the tip of an undercutting rib to create a rough surface (photo A). Add a drop or two of water to the scored area to create a tacky surface.

3 Round the base of a small triangular ball of very soft clay. Press the rounded surface of the clay ball onto the scored surface of the lid (photo B). Add enough water to work the clay, but not so much that it drips down the side of the lid. With a quick wheel speed, center the clay ball on the lid and form a solid cylinder (photo C).

4 Push your fingertips in at the base to narrow the cylinder (photo D). While supporting the clay with your index

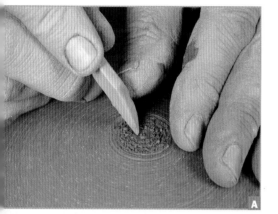

finger, push the top of the cylinder down over your index finger to flatten it (photo E). Stretch the clay outward to form the knob.

5 To make the knob easy to grasp and pick up, bevel its edge inward. Slowly slide your index finger down the edge of the knob, then gently press inward toward the base of the knob (photo F).

6 With the back of your fingernail, create a light line around the top of the knob as a decorative element (photo G). Dampen the trimmed area with a sponge, then wipe the surface of the knob and the lid clean. Burnish the trimmed area smooth with a soft rubber rib.

7 Release the lid from the trimming pad using the

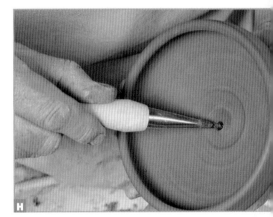

keyhole. Check the rim to make sure it's clean. If there is any residual clay from the pad on the rim, wipe it clean with a damp sponge or your fingertips.

8 On the underside of the lid, cut a small hole in the center with a tapered hole cutter (photo H). This air hole releases steam from the thick knob during firing. Without the air hole, the knob could explode in the kiln when the lid is fired. Set the lid on a wareboard to air-dry until bone dry.

FIRING, WAXING, & GLAZING

1 When the two pieces are bone dry, load them into the kiln for the first firing. Fire the lid in place on the base of the butter dish to keep both pieces round.

2 Fire the bisque kiln to approximately 1750° Fahrenheit for about 10 to 12 hours. When the bisque kiln has cooled to 200° Fahrenheit or less, it's ready to open.

3 With a narrow foam brush, apply wax-resist emulsion to the base of the butter dish and the areas where the lid and base will touch. Rotating the pieces on a banding wheel while applying the wax emulsion guarantees an even wax line.

4 Make sure to wax the rim of the lid, including the interior edge (photo A), the neck of the base, and the corner where the neck meets the outside ledge. Wax an ample area so if the lid shifts when it's firing in the kiln, the glazed surfaces won't kiss and stick to the base of the butter dish (photo B). Set the pieces aside to dry for about ten minutes. The wax emulsion should be dry to the touch before proceeding.

5 To glaze the butter dish, select two complementary glaze colors. Stir the first glaze to mix up any particles that may have settled to the bottom. This is the base glaze; it will be the dominant color of the butter dish.

6 Dip the base in the first glaze, holding on to the waxed areas where possible. Keep the pot submerged for about three seconds. Then place the piece on a clean wareboard. Immediately touch up the areas where you held the dish during the dip. Use your finger or a small, soft brush to dab glaze over the bare clay (photo C).

7 Dip the lid in the first glaze color for about three seconds. Again, hold the waxed areas as you dip the pot to limit the amount of touching up. Place the lid onto a clean wareboard, immediately touching up the bare spots of clay with a dab of glaze. When the sheen has gone off the pots, the first layer of glaze is dry. Clean the waxed areas with a damp sponge to remove any excess glaze beads that might have adhered to the waxed surfaces (photo D).

8 Place the lid on the banding wheel, making sure that the banding wheel surface is clean and free of wax emulsion and glaze. With a sharp-tipped brush, apply a few decorative lines of wax emulsion on top of the glazed surface. By spinning the lid on the banding wheel quickly while you paint, you'll get an even circle and a neat decorating line (photo E).

9 Place the decorative wax lines where the lid changes shape to highlight these changes. Also add a swirl to the top of the knob (photo F). Let the wax lines dry completely before the next step; if the wax is sticky, it's not dry.

10 Stir up the second glaze thoroughly. Turn the lid upside down and hold it inside by the rim. Dip it into the second glaze color for one or two seconds (photo G). Let the lid and base of the dish air-dry until they are completely dry, which takes about ten minutes.

11 Load the pieces into the kiln for the glaze firing. Fire the lid in place on the base of the butter dish to keep both pieces true. The kiln should fire to cone 6, or about 2200° Fahrenheit, for about 10 to 12 hours. Let the kiln cool for an additional 36 hours before unloading it. If the lid is stuck to the base after firing, a gentle tap should separate them.

Butter Dish Glaze Recipe

The primary glaze is Raspberry Red. It's a glossy glaze fired to cone 6 in oxidation. The secondary glaze is Cream Rust. It's also a glossy glaze fired to cone 6 in oxidation. With a thick application, it's cream. With a thin application, the cream breaks rust-red on the edges and textured areas of the pot.

RASPBERRY RED:		CREAM RUST:	
Nepheline Syenite	18.0%	Custer Feldspar	26.6%
Ferro Frit #3134	14.0%	Strontium Carbonate	3.3%
Whiting	20.0%	Ferro Frit #3134	30.6%
OM-4 Ball Clay	18.0%	Wollastonite	10.6%
Silica	30.0%	Talc	2.3%
	100.0%	EPK	8.4%
ADD:		Silica	18.2%
Chrome Oxide	0.20%		100.0%
Tin Oxide	3.75%	**ADD:**	
		Red Iron Oxide	6.00%
		Tin Oxide 13.00	1.90%

ADDITIONAL KNOBS

Any shape that's aesthetically pleasing as well as functional — one you can grasp easily and use to pick up the lid — will work well on this lid. Using different knob treatments expands the variety of butter dishes you can produce, adding to your palette as a potter.

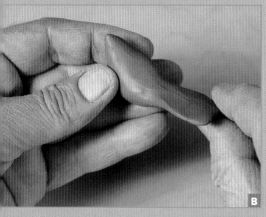

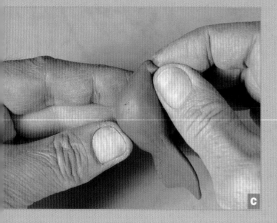

SCULPTED BIRD KNOB

1 To make a sculpted bird knob, start with a 1-ounce ball of very soft clay. Work the ball between your fingers to elongate it, forming a football shape (photo A, top left).

2 Pinch each end of the football shape to form the tail (photo B, center left) and the head of the bird. Take a very tiny piece of clay — about the size of two pinheads — and roll it into a cone shape to form the bird's beak. Attach the beak to the bird's head (photo C, bottom left).

3 Wet the scored area of the lid with water. Let it soak until the top of the lid is tacky, then gently press the base of the bird onto the scored area of the lid. Wiggle the bird back and forth to secure the attachment, and be careful not to squash the bird as you press it onto the lid.

TEXTURED COIL KNOB

1 To make a textured coil knob, start with a 6-ounce ball of soft clay. Roll a uniform clay coil about 3/4˝ in diameter and 3˝ long. Then roll the coil between two textured boards or textured rubber mats to make a pattern on the clay (photo A, below).

2 Cut each end of the coil on a bevel so the knob is about 2˝ long (photo B, opposite page, top). Wet the top of the lid with water and let it soak in until the surface is tacky. Center the coil on the lid, then gently press it onto the tacky surface.

3 Secure the knob onto the lid by pressing each end down firmly with a wooden dowel, moving the dowel back and forth in a rocking motion (photo C, opposite page, top). Smooth the ends of the knob with a damp sponge to finish.

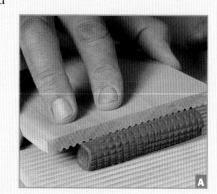

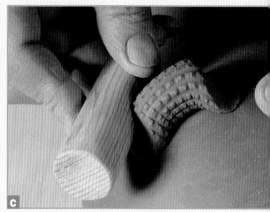

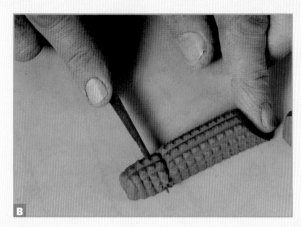

THROWN AND CUT KNOB

1 To make a thrown and cut knob, roll a piece of very soft clay into a ball about 1″ in diameter. Wet the center of the lid with a damp sponge, then press the ball of clay onto the center of the lid (photo A).

2 Using a quick wheel speed, center the ball of clay into a dome shape. Further define the shape and smooth the surface of the dome with a wooden rib (photo B).

3 Stop the wheel, then cut away one-third of the clay from each side of the dome. Using a taught cut-off wire or a wire knife, make the cut with a curved motion (photo C).

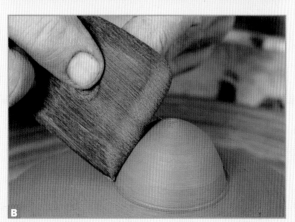

4 Let the knob dry until it is soft-leather hard. Cut a hole through the center of the knob with a tapered hole cutter (photo D).

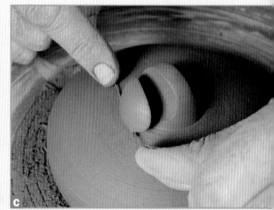

Wheel-Thrown Pottery

3

Advanced Projects

Throwing clay is all about developing skills. As you master each one, your confidence increases. Before you know it, you're able to manipulate complex forms with ease. The advanced projects in this chapter build on your knowledge of throwing simple shapes. You'll make an oval baking dish from a round form, then combine a bowl and goblet to make a dip bowl. You'll learn to make a simple lid for a garlic jar before creating snug-fitting lids for lidded boxes. The marbled vase teaches you how to combine different colors of clay at the wheel. And finally, you'll turn a tall cylindrical form into a balanced and graceful pitcher with large-scale handles.

OVAL BAKING DISH

The glossy glaze of this baking dish makes it oven-proof and easy to clean, as well as microwave and dishwasher safe. Overall, it's one of the most practical pieces of pottery I make for the kitchen.

◢◢◢ PROJECT SUMMARY ◢◢◢

The oval baker introduces another basic wheel-thrown shape — the cylinder. Although the baker is ovoid when finished, it begins as a short, wide, and cylindrical form. A couple of precise cuts in the base and a bit of further manipulation transforms this round dish into an oval. I've added a sturdy, rolled rim and coiled handles to make the dish attractive as well as practical; it works well as both a baking dish and a serving piece.

You Will Need

Materials:

- 1 pound ball of clay (for the handles)
- 2½ pound ball of clay (for the dish)
- 2 pound ball of clay (for the trimming pad)
- Wax-resist emulsion
- Bucket of water
- Two contrasting glazes

- Rounded wooden dowel
- Wallpaper seam roller
- Pointed wooden sculpting tool
- Two texturing boards
- Pointed wooden rib
- Soft rubber rib

Tools:

- Bat
- Banding wheel
- Small ware board
- Ruler
- Fettling knife

- Stiff rubber rib
- Looped trimming tool
- Cut-off wire
- Small sponge
- Narrow foam brush
- Signature stamp (optional)

THROWING THE DISH

1 To make an oval baking dish on the potter's wheel, weigh out three lumps of clay: 2½ pounds, 2 pounds, and 1 pound. Knead each piece thoroughly to remove air pockets.

2 Attach a bat to the wheel head. Center the 2½-pound ball of clay on the bat, using a fast wheel speed and plenty of water. Now open the clay, moving your fingertips parallel to the wheel head as you pull and draw the clay outward to the 4 or 5 o'clock position on the wheel head. The inside floor of the dish should be flat when finished.

3 Run the fingertips of both hands back and forth from the center to the outer edge of the clay several times to compress the base. This compression strengthens the floor and helps the dish withstand the thermal shock of going in and out of the oven.

4 The base of this piece should be made thicker than that of a normal dish; it should measure a little less than ½″ thick. (For instructions on how to measure the thickness of the base refer to page 34, step 8).

5 When the inside floor of the dish is 6″ in diameter, begin to pull the wall of the cylinder upward. Make sure to use plenty of water so the clay glides easily beneath your fingers.

6 To pull the wall, first tuck the tip of your thumb under the outside base of the thick wall to create a deep groove (photo A, following page). Then tuck the tips of your middle and ring fingers into the groove and slide the clay upward from the base to the rim. Keep the fingertips of your other hand inside the pot, opposite the outside fingertips, as you pull the clay upward (photo B, following page).

7 Keep the rim thick. As you reach the top with each pull, capture the clay between your fingertips, then place your thumb across the top of the rim and compress the clay slightly. Limiting the rise of the wall in this manner ensures a strong, thick rim (photo C, following page).

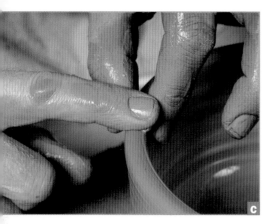

8 At regular intervals during the pulling step, reposition the wall so it remains upright. To do this, place the fingers and palms of both hands on the outside of the wall at the 12 o'clock position on the wheel head. Gently pull and coax the clay toward you to straighten the wall and counteract the centrifugal force of the wheel. Continue to pull the wall upward until it measures 3½″ tall.

9 Create a rolled rim by stopping your fingertips short of the rim as you make the last pull on the wall. Use the side of your thumb tip to create a groove just below the rim at the top outside edge of the cylinder. Then move the clay from inside the rim to the outside, rolling it over the side of your thumb. Use your inside fingertips to gently round the rim as you roll it outward (photo D).

10 With a ruler, measure the diameter of the dish; it should be about 8″ from rim to rim. The wall of the dish will be leaning outward slightly, as there should be a distance of about 1″ from the base to the rim.

11 Use a soft rubber rib to smooth the inside floor of the dish. It's important to round and soften the inside corner where the wall meets the floor. If the corner is angled sharply, stress will develop at this point and the dish could crack when it's heated repeatedly in the oven.

12 Clean up the inside of the baking dish and remove the excess water with a sponge. Then sponge the rim to soften it, remove any excess slip, and better define its round, rolled shape.

13 With the short side of a wooden rib, smooth and finish the shape of the outside wall. Keep one hand inside the dish, fingertips opposite the tool, to support the wet clay as you press the rib against the wall.

14 Cut a shallow bevel at the base of the dish with the tip of an undercutting stick.

15 With the sharp tip of a wooden rib or an undercutting stick, create a decorative line on the inside rim. Support the rim on the outside with damp fingertips placed opposite the tool, then press the tip into the clay just below and inside the rounded rim (photo E). Lightly sponge the rim again to soften the line and remove any burrs left by the tool.

16 When the outside wall of the dish is smooth, use the tip of a wooden rib to create another decorative line. Position the point of the rib about one-third of the way down the wall. As the pot slowly rotates, press the tip of the tool into the wall to create a straight line. When the pot has rotated about three-quarters of the way around on the wheel head, wiggle the rib. This loose flowing line will be part straight, part wavy, and will make an attractive focal point on the outside of the dish (photo F).

17 Do not cut the dish free from the bat yet. Remove the bat from the wheel head and set it aside to air-dry until the dish is soft-leather hard. Soft-leather hard means the surface is no longer tacky and the clay is pliable enough to bend without cracking.

FORMING THE OVAL SHAPE

1 Now it's time to alter the shape of the dish from round to oval. This takes several steps and a couple of unique tools, including a small wallpaper roller and a pointed sculpting tool.

2 With the tip of a sculpting tool, make a light mark at the center of the base. Then mark two more spots ¾″ above and below this center mark (photo A).

3 Cut completely through the floor of the pot with the sculpting tool. Cut from the point above center to the point below center, creating a leaf-shaped crescent. The thickness of the tool's tip will separate the crescent from the base (photo B, following page).

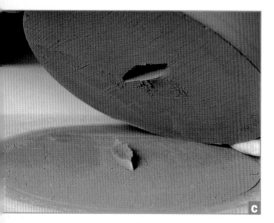

4 Pull the cut-off wire under the pot using the bevel at the base as a guide. Then, using the rounded end of the sculpting tool or a fingertip, press down on the clay crescent to stick it firmly to the bat.

5 Place your hands near the base and hold the dish firmly as you peel it from the bat. The crescent of clay should remain on the bat (photo C). Set the dish onto a clean, dry, and flat surface.

6 Now press the dish into an oval shape (photo D). First, position your palms and fingertips evenly on the wall of the dish near its base, then gently squeeze the sides together to close the crescent. To produce an even oval shape, rotate the dish as you squeeze it so all of the compression doesn't happen at one end.

7 When the seam is closed — or almost closed — press the edges of the crescent together. Use the rounded end of a wooden dowel and firmly press into the closed crescent repeatedly. This seals the crescent completely and creates a deep depression inside the center of the dish. As you close the seam, be sure not to press the tip of the dowel through the floor of the dish (photo E).

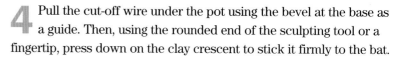

TIPS | DIY Network Crafts

For a smooth signature on the baking dish, or any piece of pottery, use a sturdy 3″ x 3″ piece of pliable plastic and the end of a pointed stick to sign your name. The plastic prevents burrs from forming at the edges of your signature as it would if you were to scratch directly into the clay. For the plastic, a piece of wrapping from a bag of prepared clay is ideal. Use a sharp pencil (but not so sharp it will puncture the plastic) or the tip of a pointed tool to write with. Place the plastic over the area where you want to sign, and then write your name on the plastic with the tip of the stick.

8 Roll the clay crescent left on the bat into a small tapered coil. Use a fingertip to press the coil into the seam's depression, and then close the sides of the seam against the coil (photo F).

9 Compress the coil into the seam with a small wallpaper roller or a stiff rubber rib. Work the roller vertically and horizontally over the seam until the base is even and the floor of the dish is smooth and level (photo G). When finished, use a damp sponge to further smooth the floor of the dish.

E

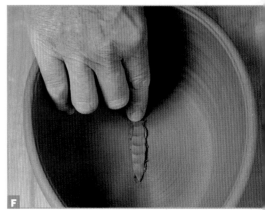

F

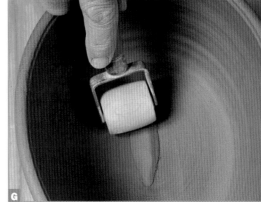

G

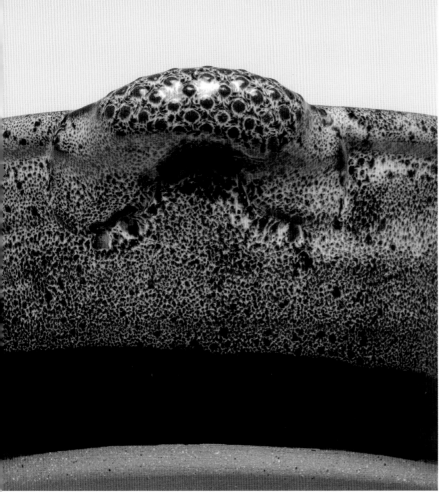

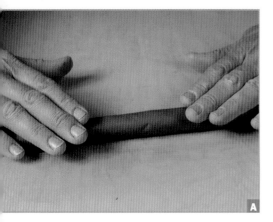

MAKING THE HANDLES

1 To make handles for the dish, roll out a coil of clay about 1/2″ in diameter and 6″ to 8″ long. To roll a uniform coil, first position your hands on the clay with fingertips pointed inward and spread wide. Relax your hands, press lightly on the clay, then roll from the center of the coil outward to the ends, and then back to center again. Roll until the coil is the correct thickness (photo A).

2 Use a fettling knife to cut two 3″ pieces of coil from the long coil. Add texture to the coils by rolling them between two textured surfaces. Many kinds of texturing tools will work, but the best ones — such as wood, cardboard, and dry plastic — have surfaces to which the clay won't stick. In this example, two corrugated boards held at different angles were used (photo B).

3 Wet the ends of the dish thoroughly just below the rim with a sponge. With dry fingertips, soften the ends of the coils by rolling them gently between your fingertips (photo C).

4 Bend one coil into an arched shape and place it against the dampened side of the dish just below the rim. The U-shaped coil should be upside down so that its top is level with the rim and the two ends are below the rim.

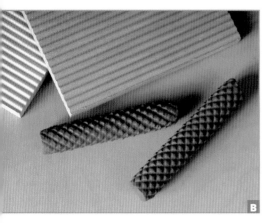

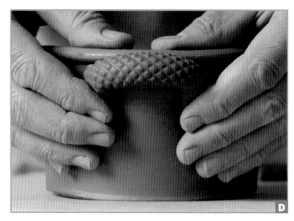

5 Gently press the handle onto the dish with your fingertips, supporting the rim with your thumb tips positioned inside the dish. Use your fingertips to press the handle firmly to the outside wall (photo D). Once attached, tilt the handle slightly upward so its top is just above the rim (photo E). Attach the other coil handle to the opposite end of the dish the same way.

6 Use a short piece of wooden dowel to secure the handles firmly to the sides of the dish. Roll the dowel back and forth across the ends of the handles, pressing and flattening the ends to the outside wall. Support the inside wall with your fingertips opposite the tool as you work (photo F). When finished, set the dish aside to air-dry until it's stiff-leather hard.

E

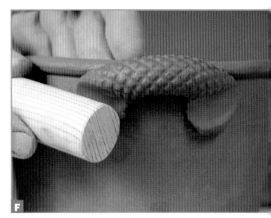

F

TRIMMING THE BASE

1 To trim the base of the baking dish, first throw a clay trimming pad. (See page 38, step 2 for instructions on how to make a trimming pad.)

2 With a looped trimming tool, cut away both sides of the trimming pad to accommodate the dish's handles. Because the handles sit above the rim, it's not possible to place the dish upside down without damaging them. By cutting away the sides of the pad, the handles are suspended and protected above the wheel head (photo A).

A

3 Center the dish upside down on the trimming pad, making sure the handles don't touch the pad or the wheel head (photo B). Rotate the wheel slowly to trim the base.

4 Use the straight edge of the looped trimming tool to gently trim away the sharp corner at the base of the dish. Let the tool float over the clay — even though it feels a bit odd to trim this oval shape, be patient and let the tool flow naturally (photo C).

5 For a rounded bevel that mimics the curved inside edge of the dish, lightly trim the base about ½″ up the side. The bevel on the bottom of the dish should be a bit less than 1″ wide overall. Wet the trimmed area with a damp sponge, then burnish the dampened area with a soft rubber rib.

6 When finished, sign the piece on the base or press your chop, or signature stamp, into the side of the dish near the foot. Place the dish upright on a clean, dry surface. Let it air-dry until it is bone dry.

TIPS | DIY Network Crafts

If the coil you roll for the handles becomes flat or squared, it means you're pressing down too hard on the coil or you're not rolling the coil over the surface of the table far enough.

FIRING, WAXING, & GLAZING

1 Load the dish into the kiln for the first firing. Fire the bisque kiln to approximately 1750° Fahrenheit for about 10 to 12 hours. When the kiln has cooled to 200° Fahrenheit or less, it's ready to open.

2 Apply wax-resist emulsion to the base of the dish. To protect the handles and keep the dish level, elevate it on a banding wheel. Then use a narrow foam brush to apply the wax onto the base of the baking dish.

3 Wax the entire trimmed bevel, including the beveled area that extends up the side of the dish. Then apply wax across the base (photo A). Let the wax air-dry until it is dry to the touch.

4 To glaze the oval baking dish, select two contrasting and compatible glaze colors. Stir up the base glaze, mixing all of the suspended particles. Now hold the dish with two fingers at the rim, submerging it completely into the glaze for three seconds (photo B).

5 Place the dish on a clean surface. Immediately touch up the bare clay with a dab of glaze and your fingertip or a soft, pointed brush.

6 Let the glaze dry until the sheen has left the pot. Once dry, clean the waxed area with a damp sponge to remove any glaze that might have adhered to the base.

7 Now stir up the second glaze. Clean your hands before making the second dip to avoid contaminating this glaze with the first glaze.

8 Hold the dish upside down with a thumb on one side and your middle and ring fingers on the other side. (Use two hands if one isn't big enough to span the bottom of the dish.) Make sure to place two fingers on one side of the dish and one or two fingers on the other side. This finger position creates an interesting line on the outside wall where the second glaze ends.

9 Carefully dip the upside down and level dish into the glaze for one or two seconds. Be sure to submerge three-fourths of the pot so at least ½″ of your fingertips are covered in glaze (photo C).

TIPS | DIY Network Crafts

A sturdy, even wall and base thickness is very important when throwing ovenware. As the ware goes in and out of the oven, the heat is distributed throughout the walls and base of the pot. A baking dish can better withstand the thermal shock and extreme temperature swings without cracking if the thickness of the wall and base are equal and uniform.

10 Hold the dish upside down over the glaze bucket for about 10 seconds, or until all the drips have dried. Place the dish right side up on a clean, dry surface, and then load it into the kiln once it has air-dried thoroughly.

11 Fire the glaze kiln to cone 6, or about 2200° Fahrenheit, for about 10 to 12 hours. Let the kiln cool for an additional 36 hours before unloading it.

12 Take your baking dish to the kitchen, fill it with your favorite casserole, and pop it in the oven or the microwave. When it's done, take it to the table with pride. It looks great!

Oval Baking Dish Glaze Recipe

The primary glaze is Black Licorice. It's a glossy glaze fired to cone 6 in oxidation. The secondary glaze is Cream Rust. It's also a glossy fired to cone 6 in oxidation. With a thick application, it's cream. With a thin application, the cream breaks rust-red on the edges and textured areas of the pot.

BLACK LICORICE:		CREAM RUST:	
Custer Feldspar	22.0%	Custer Feldspar	26.6%
Whiting	4.0%	Strontium Carbonate	3.3%
Talc	5.0%	Ferro Frit #3134	30.6%
EPK	17.0%	Wollastonite	10.6%
Silica	26.0%	Talc	2.3%
Ferro Frit #3134	26.0%	EPK	8.4%
	100.0%	Silica	18.2%
			100.0%
ADD:			
Cobalt Carbonate	1.0%	**ADD:**	
Red Iron Oxide	9.0%	Red Iron Oxide	6.00%
Bentonite	2.0%	Tin Oxide	13.00

HANDLE VARIATION

By altering the style of handles, you can change the look and feel of this oval baking dish. It's important to attach handles that are functionally sound, so pick the right variation with care. Remember, when the baking dish is full and hot, you'll need to be able to pick it up easily with bulky oven mitts. One alternative style of handle that's both attractive and practical is the tapered-coil handle.

1 To make this style of handle, roll out a coil 6″ to 8″ in length. Use a fettling knife to cut the coil into two matching 3″ lengths. Roll and taper each end of both coils to a soft point (photo A).

2 Use a sponge to wet each end of the dish just below the rim on the outside wall. Apply the water liberally so the handles will stick well. Bend each handle into a U-shaped arch, then press them onto the side of the dish. Place one at each end just below the rim.

3 With wet fingertips, stroke and press each coil securely to the wall (photo B). Then bend the pointed ends inward and under the handle. Use the side of your thumb to swipe the end of each handle downward, securing the ends to the wall (photo C). Use a damp sponge to soften the edges and the surrounding area where the handles attached to the dish.

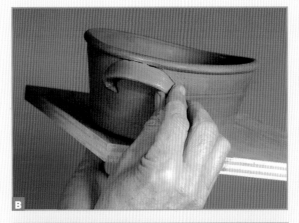

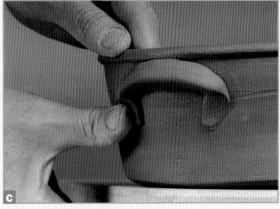

DIP BOWL

This clever dip bowl looks great and is very functional — it keeps dip at the right temperature, whether it's cool or warm. The bowl is a two-piece set that holds either ice or hot water in the base and dip in the top. I designed it so when the two parts are nested together they appear as a single, elegant piece.

◀◀ PROJECT SUMMARY ▶▶

To begin, I make the base section first; it's a simple cylinder with a thick, sturdy rim. Then I make a wide-rimmed bowl that fits into the top of the cylinder. I trim each piece and add a pair of textured handles to the base, making it easy to carry. Summer or winter, this dip server will be a great addition to your next party.

You Will Need

Materials:

- 2½-pound ball of clay (for the cylinder)
- 1¼-pound ball of clay (for the bowl)
- 1 pound of clay (for handles and trimming pad)
- Wax-resist emulsion
- Two complementary glazes
- Bucket of water

Tools:

- Bat
- Wareboard
- Banding wheel
- Ruler
- Pointed wooden rib
- Soft rubber rib
- Needle tool
- Looped trimming tool
- Short piece of wooden dowel
- Texturing tools
- Cut-off wire (or a wavy "wiggle wire")
- Wide scraper
- Fettling knife
- Rolling pin
- Two ½″ thick slats
- Small sponge
- Foam brush
- Signature stamp (optional)

⫸ THROWING THE BASE ⫷

1 To begin this project, weigh out a 2½-pound ball of clay for the cylinder, or base, of the set. Weigh out a 1¼-pound ball for the bowl, or top part of the set. This makes a two-piece set that's 6½″ wide when wet. Knead each piece thoroughly to remove air pockets and to homogenize the clay completely.

2 Make the cylindrical base of the set first. Begin by attaching a bat to the wheel head so the wet pot can later be removed from the wheel without being damaged. It's essential that the cylinder remain perfectly round through all steps so the bowl will fit inside of it.

3 Rotate the base of the 2½-pound lump of clay on a clean, dry surface to compress and smooth the bottom of the ball. This makes for a firm, air-free attachment between the clay and the bat (photo A). Slap the ball of clay firmly onto the center of the bat.

4 Center the clay on the wheel head using a fast wheel speed and plenty of water. If needed, refer to the Basics chapter for extra directions on centering the clay. While centering the clay, keep your hands firmly on the form and your elbows firmly on your thighs or against the wheel tray. The steadier you are in this position, the easier it will be to center the clay.

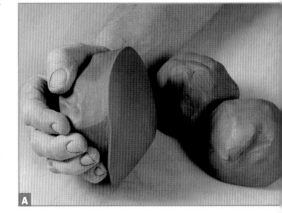

A

B

5 Place your palms and fingers on either side of the clay ball, then cross your thumbs over each other and across the top of the clay (photo B, previous page). Press inward from both sides and down from the top with equal pressure. Add water as needed to wet the clay so it slides easily beneath your fingers and palms as you work. If the clay wobbles as the wheel spins, it's not centered. A centered piece of clay will spin smoothly on the wheel head with no side-to-side motion.

6 Next, open the clay (refer to the Basics chapter if needed) by pressing your fingertips down into the center of the clay while supporting the outside edge with your thumbs (photo C). Use your fingertips to draw the clay outward a couple of inches. The thickness of the bottom, or floor, of the pot should be about ¼″. Make the inside floor of the pot flat by keeping your fingertips parallel to the wheel head. The beginning of the cylindrical form should now be taking shape.

7 Before opening the form any further, measure the thickness of the floor using a needle tool (see page 34, step 8 for directions on using the needle tool). When the base is about ¼˝ thick, continue to open the clay. Spread the clay to about 7˝, or a bit wider than the size of the finished pot.

8 Pull the wall of the form upward using a medium wheel speed and lots of water (see Basics chapter, if needed). If you feel the clay getting out of control as you pull, slow the wheel down. As you begin to draw the wall upward, move it inward as well, creating a tight, angled corner inside the pot where the base meets the wall (photo D). If necessary, use the palms of both hands to gently collar in the cylinder to keep the walls vertical.

9 There are a few things to keep in mind as you pull the wall. Before each pull, tuck the tip of your right thumb under the outside of the form at the bottom of the wall, then push a groove in the base (photo E). Keep the middle fingers wet as you tuck them into the groove beneath the wall to make each pull.

10 As you pull the wall, keep the fingertips of your other hand positioned inside the pot, opposite the outside fingertips. Keeping your hands connected above the rim for stability, move both hands together to slowly pull the clay upward. After each pull, level and strengthen the rim by placing a fingertip on the inside of the rim, a thumb tip outside of the rim, and a fingertip on top of the rim. Compressing the clay firmly at these three points creates a strong, level rim, which is especially important on this piece (photo F).

11 Once the wall has been pulled, measure the form. The outside diameter of the cylinder should now measure 6½˝ across, while the inside diameter should measure 6˝. The rim should then be ¼˝ thick and the height of the cylinder should be 4½˝ tall. If it's too short, make another pull or two until it's the correct height.

12 When the cylinder is the correct size, use the straight edge of a wooden rib to smooth and straighten the outside wall. Press the flat side of the wooden rib against the wall while supporting the clay on the inside with your other hand (photo G).

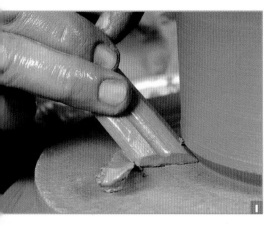

13 Define the rim by using the corner of the rib to press a slightly beveled groove just below the rim on the outside edge of the cylinder. This is a waxing guideline that will be used later during the glazing process (photo H, previous page). Remove any excess water from inside the cylinder and smooth the rim with a small sponge.

14 Press the point of a wooden rib or the tip of an undercutting stick against the bat and into the foot of the cylinder. With the wheel turning at medium speed, cut a ½″ deep groove around the outside base (photo I). This groove will guide the cut-off wire as you separate the pot from the bat.

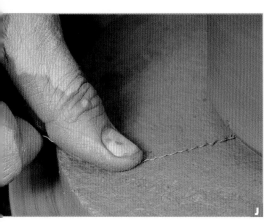

15 Now stop the wheel. To make a wavy pattern on the base of the pot, wiggle the cut-off wire while pulling it under the cylinder (photo J). The wiggled wire and a wavy hand motion will make a unique pattern on the bottom of the pot. Carefully remove the bat from the wheel head with the cylinder attached, then set it aside to air-dry.

TIPS | DIY Network Crafts

Be careful when preparing and measuring the floor of a piece. If the bottom of a pot is thrown too thin, it can crack when in use or when "shocked" by hot water. If the bottom is thrown too thick, you'll have to trim away a lot of clay from the base, or the pot will be too heavy.

◀◀ THROWING THE BOWL ▶▶

1 The next step is to make the top piece of the project, which is the bowl. This bowl can be thrown without a bat on the wheel head because it is small and has a narrow foot. It will be easy to lift from the wheel head using a simple tool and your fingertips.

2 Rotate the base of the second ball of clay on a clean, dry surface to smooth and compress the bottom. This step ensures a tight seal between the clay and the wheel head. Once the clay is prepared, slap it firmly onto the middle of the wheel head and sprinkle it with plenty of water.

3 With a fast wheel speed, center the clay. As you pull the clay outward to open the bowl, relax the downward pressure. This action creates a gentle curve inside the bottom of the form, beginning the shape of the bowl.

4 Now, using a medium wheel speed and plenty of water, make one pull upward and slightly outward on the wall. Before making the second pull, press the tip of your thumb into and under the outside base of the wall to create a ½˝ deep groove. Tuck two wet fingertips into the groove. Place the fingertips of your other hand inside the pot, opposite and slightly above your outside fingertips. Slowly pull the wall of clay upward, moving the clay from the bottom to the top of the bowl to create a thick, heavy rim.

5 Pull the wall of the bowl up and outward until it's 3½˝ tall and a bit less than 6˝ wide. The dimensions of the bowl are very important, so measure often and with care. The bowl has to be short enough to ensure that its base won't touch the inside floor of the cylinder when they're nested together.

6 Stop the last pull ½˝ below the rim. When the bowl is the right height, widen and flatten the rim between your fingertips. As you pull the clay out, keep your right thumb pressed on top of the rim as you flatten and widen it. The bottom side of this wide rim will rest on the rim of the cylinder.

7 Use a ruler to measure across the top of the bowl. The outside diameter should be 6¾˝ across, or just a bit wider than the cylinder. If the bowl is too wide, gently collar it in using both palms positioned at 12 o'clock on the wheel head (photo A). If the bowl is too narrow, widen it with another gentle pull. Using a slow to medium wheel speed, remove the water from the inside of the bowl with a small sponge.

8 Now add some decorative flourishes. Supporting beneath the rim with your fingertips, use the sharp tip of a wooden rib to gently score some shallow lines into the flat-topped area of the bowl's rim (photo B). Lightly sponge the rim to smooth the lines.

9 You can also add a decorative swirl at the inside center of the bowl. Place a fingertip about an inch from the middle of the bowl, then gently swipe it across the center as the pot rotates slowly on the wheel head (photo C). These decorative flourishes will pool the glaze and create an interesting, three-dimensional detail (photo D).

10 Take final measurements, making sure the bowl is the correct width and height — 3½″ tall and 6¾″ wide. With the wooden rib, press a groove into the base and against the wheel head, then cut the bowl free from the wheel head with the wiggle wire.

11 To remove the bowl from the wheel, place a wet, wide scraper onto the wheel head next to the foot of the bowl. With dry fingertips, gently pry the foot up ½″ and place the scraper under the base of the bowl. Set the base onto the wet scraper and lift the bowl from the wheel head to a clean, dry wareboard. Quickly pull the scraper away. As you pry the bowl from the wheel head and set it on the scraper, the bowl will become oval shaped at the rim. However, as you quickly pull the scraper from beneath the base of the bowl to place it on the wareboard, the rim will move back into round. In fact, using this technique to lift the bowl from the wheel head ensures that the bowl stays perfectly round (photos E and F).

12 Set both pieces of the project aside to dry until they are leather hard. Drying time depends on the humidity and airflow in your studio. You can accelerate the drying process by placing pots in front of a fan or under a heat lamp. But be careful — dry them evenly and don't let them get too dry too fast.

TIPS | DIY Network Crafts

Don't overload your brush with wax emulsion. An overloaded brush, when pressed against a pot, can cause the wax to drip and run down the walls. If this happens, the glaze won't stick or cover the waxed surface. Your only option is to bisque fire the piece again and start the waxing process over.

TRIMMING THE CYLINDER AND BOWL

1 When the pieces are leather hard, they're ready to trim. To keep from damaging the rims, trim the pieces on a clay or foam rubber pad. (See page 38, step 2 for directions on how to make a clay trimming pad.)

2 Invert the cylinder and center it on the trimming pad. If using a clay pad, press down on the cylinder gently to ensure a strong attachment between the rim and the pad.

3 With a looped trimming tool and a quick wheel speed, trim the excess clay from the bottom edge of the cylinder. Hold the pot in place by pressing down lightly in the center of the base, using your thumb to stabilize the trimming tool. Then rotate the tool as you trim to create a rounded profile at the foot of the cylinder (photo A).

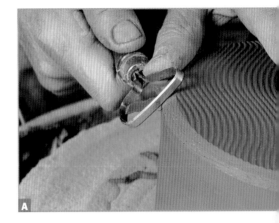

4 When you've finished trimming, smooth the cut surface with a damp sponge. Then burnish the damp, trimmed area with the edge of a soft rubber rib to push the aggregate (or sand) raised by the trimming tool back into the clay.

5 To frame the wiggle wire pattern on the base of the cylinder, use the side of your fingernail or the sharp tip of a wooden rib to make a shallow groove surrounding the wiggled lines (photo B). When finished, soften the line with a damp sponge.

6 Now stop the wheel, grasp the cylinder at its base, and pop it free from the pad. Placing your hands at the base rather than at the top will keep the rim round. Set the cylinder onto a clean, dry wareboard.

7 Next, trim the bowl. First, use the straight side of a wooden rib to clean and level the clay trimming pad. Then use your thumb to create a keyhole at the edge of the clay pad. This keyhole allows you release the bowl from the pad when you're finished trimming.

8 Test the bowl for size and fit by placing it very gently into the cylinder. Note how much clay you'll need to trim from the underside of the bowl's rim to create a snug fit between the two pieces. Remove the bowl from the cylinder, then invert it and center it on the trimming pad. Press down on the bowl lightly to ensure a strong attachment to the pad.

9 With a medium wheel speed, use the narrow end of the trimming tool to reach into the corner of the rim and trim away a small amount of clay. When finished, stop the wheel, pick up the bowl, and test it again for fit by placing it back in the cylinder. If needed, continue to trim in small amounts, measuring often, until the bowl fits into the cylinder with a little room to spare. If it's too tight, the cylinder will trap the bowl when it shrinks during the glaze firing.

10 When the bowl and cylinder fit perfectly, trim the foot of the bowl. With a trimming tool and a medium to fast wheel speed, trim the excess clay from the bottom of the bowl. The diameter of the flat base will be quite small — about 1½″. Shape the wall of the bowl by trimming a gentle curve from the corner under the rim to the foot (photo C). Dampen the surface with a sponge, then use a rubber rib to smooth and burnish the surface.

11 Remove the bowl from the trimming pad. Make sure the rim is clean and dry. Place the bowl on a clean wareboard to air-dry.

◀◀ ATTACHING THE HANDLES ▶▶

1 Next, make two handles and attach them to the cylinder. To begin, prepare a dry, clean surface on which to work. Start with a coil of clay, rolling the coil across your work surface until it's about ½″ in diameter and 6″ long (photo A). Use a fettling knife to cut two handles from the coil, each about 2½″ in length (photo B).

2 Emboss a texture onto each handle by rolling the coils, one at a time, between two textured mats or corrugated boards (photo C). Trim the two pieces again until they are of equal length (photo D).

3 To attach the handles to the cylinder, first use a sponge to dampen the two handle areas, which should be opposite each other and just below the rim. Pick up one of the handles and round the ends by rolling it gently between your fingertips. Bend the handle into an arched or U shape (photo E, following page). Then place the first handle onto the dampened area just below the rim of the cylinder, lightly pressing the ends to the wall of the pot with your thumbs (photo F, following page).

4 To place the second handle correctly, make a small mark with your fingernail just below the rim, directly opposite the center of the first handle. Make sure to look down on the cylinder from above as you mark it. Attach the second handle directly opposite the first handle, repeating the steps from above. Make sure the handles are attached low enough so they won't bump into the rim of the bowl when it nests in the cylinder.

5 When the two handles are in place, secure them to the cylinder. Use a short piece of wooden dowel to gently press the ends of the handles onto the wall of the pot. Place the fingertips of one hand inside the pot to support the wall as you work.

A

C

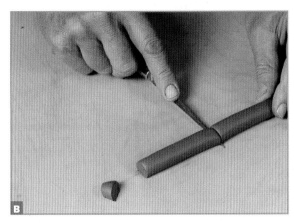

B

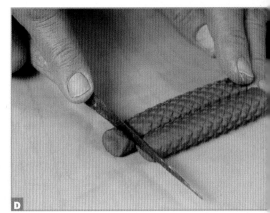

D

6 Whatever you do to one handle, match it on the other — both handles should look identical. To give the handles some visual lift, roll the dowel upward from beneath each handle (photo G). When finished, sign or initial the base of the cylinder or use your signature stamp somewhere on or near the foot (photo H).

7 Nest the bowl into the cylinder and set the pieces aside to dry completely until they are bone dry. Letting the pieces dry while nested ensures that they will stay perfectly round.

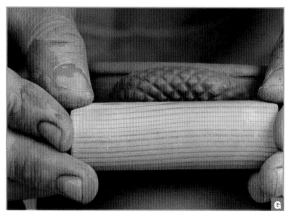

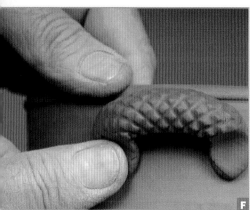

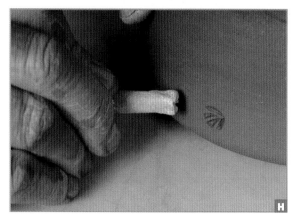

FIRING, WAXING, & GLAZING

1 Stack the still nested pieces into the kiln. Firing the pieces nested ensures the rims remain round and perfectly fitted to each other. Bisque fire the kiln to approximately 1750° Fahrenheit for 10 to 12 hours (photo A). Let the kiln cool for at least 24 hours. When the kiln has cooled to 200° Fahrenheit or less, it's ready to open.

2 Before glazing this project, apply a coat of wax-resist emulsion to the rims and base of each piece. Since the pieces will be nested during the glaze firing, the places where they touch need to be glaze-free.

3 To wax the bowl, place the cylinder upright on the banding wheel. Invert the bowl and center it on the rim of the cylinder (photo B). Using a narrow foam brush, apply wax-resist emulsion to the underside of the bowl's rim as you quickly spin the banding wheel. Also apply a straight-edged band of wax about 1/2˝ down the curved side of the bowl. Set the bowl aside for three to five minutes until the wax is dry.

4 Next, apply wax to the rim of the cylinder, waxing to the grooved guideline on the outside of the rim. Now invert the cylinder on the banding wheel. Wax across the base, working the wax emulsion into all of the wiggle wire grooves (photo C). Wax up the wall about ½˝, then set the waxed cylinder aside to dry.

5 To glaze the dip bowl, select two complementary glaze colors. Stir the first glaze, making sure it's an even consistency throughout. Hold the bowl with your fingertips at the rim and dip it into the glaze for about three seconds. Don't set it on the table when you're done — since the bottom isn't waxed putting it base down would mar the glaze. Instead, drop the bowl into the cylindrical base and let it dry there (photo D).

6 Touch up the bare patches where your fingertips held the rim. Dip a fingertip or a soft, pointed brush into the glaze and dab it where needed. Let the bowl dry for a minute or two.

7 Remove the bowl from the cylinder, set it aside, then wipe away any drips of glaze from the cylinder with a damp sponge. Hold the cylinder at the waxed areas at the rim and base, then dip it into the glaze. Submerge it completely for about three seconds, then immediately place it on the table.

8 When the glaze is dry, use a damp sponge to carefully remove any beads of glaze that remain on the waxed areas of the bowl or cylinder. Cut a sponge into a wedge-shaped triangle that will fit easily into the corners of the pots. Using this sponge will help you avoid damaging the glazed areas as you clean the pots.

9 Next, stir the second glaze thoroughly. Hold the cylinder at the base with your fingertips and quickly dip the top half into the glaze for one second. A quick dip is essential so the second layer of glaze isn't too thick (photo E). Let the second dip dry, then clean the glaze from the wax on the rim again.

10 Before dipping the bowl into the second glaze, center and invert it on the banding wheel. Wax across the glazed base and up the wall about ½″.

11 When the wax is dry, pick up the bowl. Hold it at the rim between two fingertips and dip it quickly into the second glaze. Place the bowl upright on the table, then patch the areas where your fingertips held the bowl. Clean the waxed base of the bowl with a damp sponge, then let the pieces completely air-dry.

Dip Bowl Glaze Recipe

The primary glaze is Teal Blue. It's fired to cone 6 in oxidation. The secondary glaze is Rutile Green. It's a glossy glaze and great as a thin over-dip on all cone 6 glazes.

TEAL BLUE:		RUTILE GREEN:	
Custer Feldspar	20%	Talc	5.0%
Ferro Frit #3124	20%	Custer Feldspar	22.0%
Wollastonite	20%	Whiting	4.0%
Silica	20%	Silica	26.0%
EPK	20%	Tile #6 or EPK	17.0%
	100.0%	Ferro Frit #3134	26.0%
			100.0%
ADD:			
Cobalt Carbonate	1.0%	**ADD:**	
Chrome Oxide	0.5%	Bentonite	2.0%
		Rutile (powdered)	6.0%
		Copper Carbonate	4.0%

12 Nest the two pieces together and place them into the kiln for the glaze firing. The kiln should fire to cone 6, or about 2200° Fahrenheit, for about 10 to12 hours. Let the kiln cool for an additional 36 hours before unloading it.

13 Often, the bowl and cylinder will be stuck together when you remove them from the kiln. To safely separate them, tap the center of the cylinder's base several times with a wooden stick. A firm tap or two will separate the bowl from the base. Now you're ready to serve fresh, delicious dips!

TIPS | DIY Network Crafts

Take your time and work carefully when waxing your pots. Uneven wax lines or splashes of wax in the wrong place will show up in the finished work.

TEXTURED HANDLES

There are several patterns you can use to add visual depth and texture on the handles of this dip bowl. You can use any design you like as long as the handles don't extend above the cylinder's rim and bump the bowl. Remember, it's important to have functional handles on this piece, especially since you may be carrying hot water in the base.

1 First, prepare a clean, dry space on a work table. Use very soft clay to form the handle coils. Soft clay impresses easily and distinctly.

2 Create linear patterns by arranging the corrugations of textured boards or mats par-allel to each other and the length of the coil (photo A).

3 Create a swirled pattern by arranging the corrugations of textured boards or mats at 90° to each other, then roll the coil from corner to corner between the boards (photo B).

Create a ringed pattern by arrang-ing the corrugations of the tex-tured boards or mats parallel to each other and at 90° to the coil (photo C).

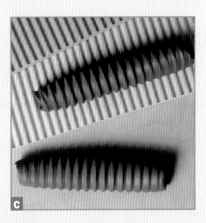

GARLIC JAR

I came across this lidded garlic jar many years ago while working as an apprentice potter in Europe. I learned that garlic stays fresh for a long time if it's stored in a dark, aerated clay pot. Since then, I've discovered other practical applications for this useful piece of pottery such as a holder for votive candles or potpourri.

◢◢◢ PROJECT SUMMARY ◢◢◢

Made on the wheel, this garlic jar begins as a cylinder. Its straight wall is "bellied out" to make the rounded shape. I then form a ledge, or gallery, at the rim of the jar to support the domed lid, which is thrown upside down off the hump. Finally, I add a knob to the top of the lid. The decorative hole pattern can be as varied as your imagination allows. Overall, this is a fun and challenging project with plenty of built-in variety for continued throwing, making, and using pleasure.

You Will Need

Materials:

- 1½-pound ball of clay (for the jar)
- 1-pound ball of clay (for the lid)
- 2-ounce ball of clay (for the knob)
- 2-pound ball of clay (for trimming pad)
- Wax-resist emulsion
- Bucket of water
- Two complementary glazes

Tools:

- Banding wheel
- Small wareboard
- Ruler
- Hole cutter
- Sculpting stick with rounded end
- Sponge on a stick
- Pointed wooden rib
- Undercutting rib
- Soft rubber rib
- Looped trimming tool
- Cut-off wire
- Small sponge
- Narrow foam brush
- Signature stamp (optional)

THROWING THE JAR

1 To prepare for throwing a garlic jar on the potter's wheel, weigh out two lumps of clay weighing 1½ pounds and 1 pound each. Knead each piece of clay thoroughly to remove air pockets. When the clay is ready, attach and center the 1½ pound ball directly onto the wheel head using a fast wheel speed and plenty of water.

2 Open the clay, making the inside base of the cylinder flat and ¼″ thick. Keep your fingers parallel to the wheel head as you spread the clay outward. Then run your fingertips back and forth from the center to the opened edge several times to compress and flatten the floor.

3 When the floor of the pot is 3 to 3½″ in diameter, begin to pull the wall of the cylinder upward. To pull the wall, first wet the clay thoroughly and slow the wheel to a medium speed. Tuck the tip of your thumb under the thick outside wall, pushing a groove under the base (photo A). Place your index and middle fingers into this groove, supporting the two fingers with your thumb.

4 Next, place the fingertips of your other hand inside the pot opposite the outside fingertips. Connect your hands by crossing your thumbs over each other lightly, then pull the clay upward (photo B).

5 Keep the rim thick and level while pulling the wall. As your fingertips reach the top of the cylinder, stop each pull just short of the rim. Capture the rim between your thumb and index finger (place the index finger inside the cylinder and the thumb outside). With the index finger or thumb of your other hand, press down on the clay to compress the rim. This action limits the rise of the wall and ensures a thick, level rim (photo C).

6 After making four or five pulls, the cylinder should be about 5″ tall. Now split the thick rim to form the gallery (or ledge) on which the lid will sit. To split the rim, begin by placing your thumb on the middle of the rim, dividing it in half. Press down with the tip of your thumb on the inside half of the rim, supporting beneath it with the fingertips of your inside hand. This action separates the rim and creates the stepped ledge known as a gallery. The gallery will be about ½″ below the top of the rim and a bit more than ¼″ wide (photo D). While working, support the outside of the rim with the fingertips of your other hand.

7 Make sure the inside edge of the gallery is substantial and rounded, not thin and sharp. If needed, use the rounded end of a sculpting tool to define and soften the angle of the gallery. Place the tool into the corner and press downward, supporting the outside rim with your fingertips as you work. This last step gives further definition to the ledge and neatens up its shape (photo E).

8 Now "belly out" the cylinder to form a rounded jar. First, place one hand inside the jar while the fingertips of your other hand support the outside wall. With a consistent, light pressure, press the clay outward to extend the belly and round out the middle of the form. As the clay expands, be sure to support it with your outside fingertips (photo F).

9 Clean up the outside surface with the straight edge of a wooden rib or the long edge of an undercutting stick to enhance the rounded belly and exterior profile of the form. Support the inside of the jar with one hand

placed opposite the tool as you work (photo G).

10 Now define the size of the jar's opening by placing the fingertips and thumbs of both hands around the jar, just below the rim (photo H). Using both hands, gently press inward with even pressure (photo I), then measure the opening with a ruler. From inside rim to inside rim, the jar should be 3½″ in diameter. Work slowly and carefully, and measure often as you reduce the diameter of the rim.

11 Remove the excess water from inside the narrow jar by using a sponge on a stick. If you don't remove the

water, the bottom will become mushy and soggy, and the pot will be ruined.

12 Use the tip of a soft sponge to smooth and soften the rim and the inside edge of the gallery. Stop the wheel when finished, then pull a cut-off wire beneath the pot. Using dry hands placed near the base on each side, lift the jar to a clean, dry wareboard.

◢◢◢ THROWING THE LID ◢◢◢

1 Now it's time to make the lid, which will be thrown "off the hump," and shaped like a shallow bowl. To form the hump, first center a 1-pound ball of clay into a cone-shaped mound directly on the wheel head. This centered hump should be about 3″ in diameter at the base, 2″ in diameter at the top, and 3″ tall (photo A).

2 Form a "doorknob" at the top of the hump by tucking the side of one hand into the clay about 1″ down from the top of the hump, then press inward (photo B).

3 To form the lid, open the doorknob by pressing your thumb tip down into the top center of the clay. Add water, then slowly pull the clay outward and slightly upward. As you draw the clay outward, relax your fingertips as they reach the edge of the lid, just as if you were throwing a bowl (photos C and D).

4 Measure the diameter of the lid several times while opening it. The wall thickness of the lid should be about the same thickness as the wall of the jar, or about ¼″. The rim of the lid should be slightly thicker than ¼″ since it has frequent contact with the jar and needs to be strong.

5 Use a ruler to measure the outside diameter of the lid again. The diameter of the lid should be exactly 3½″ when wet, which is also the same diameter as the mouth of the jar. Getting an exact final measurement is important because the lid must fit into the top of the jar snuggly.

6 When the lid is the correct diameter, use a damp sponge to soften and clean up the inside, the outside, and the rim of the form. Then, with a quick wheel speed, cut a beveled groove beneath the base of the lid with the sharp tip of a wooden rib (photo E).

7 With the wheel slowed to medium speed, place the cut-off wire into the groove and pull it quickly beneath the lid. Stop the wheel, wet your fingertips, and slide them under the lid, placing it rim up onto a clean, dry wareboard (photo F). Let both pieces dry until they're stiff-leather hard.

◀◀ TRIMMING THE JAR AND LID & ATTACHING A KNOB ▶▶

1 When both pieces are very stiff and leather hard, they're ready to trim. It's important that they're both leather hard because they'll be handled a lot at this stage. If you trim the jar when the clay is still too soft and accidentally alter its shape, the lid won't fit properly. Before trimming, test the fit by placing the lid in the gallery of the jar. If you've measured carefully, the two pieces should fit together perfectly.

2 To trim the jar and lid, throw a clay trimming pad. To begin, invert the jar onto the trimming pad, center it, and press down gently on the base to attach it securely to the pad.

3 Use the straight blade of the looped trimming tool to round and soften the edge of the foot where the side of the jar meets the base (photo A). Dampen the trimmed surface with a sponge, then use a soft rubber rib to burnish and smooth the edge of the foot. When finished, remove the jar from the pad.

4 Now prepare to trim the lid by cutting a keyhole (photo B) at the edge of the trimming pad. Without the keyhole, it would be nearly impossible to remove the flat, trimmed lid from the pad without altering its shape.

5 Place and center the lid rim down on the pad, then press down on it gently for a secure attachment. With the straight edge of the trimming tool, trim the excess clay from the top of the lid where it was cut from the hump. Mirror the interior curve of the lid as you trim the exterior surface (photo C). When finished, smooth the trimmed area with your fingertip or the edge of a soft rubber rib.

6 Before attaching the knob, score a small area with the tip of an undercutting stick by scratching concentric circles into the center of the lid. This scored area should be the same diameter as the base of the knob you're adding, which is about ¾″ in diameter. It's important that the scoring is deep and rough enough to create a surface that will securely bind the soft clay of the knob to the lid. Wet the scored area with a drop or two of water, then let the water soak in for at least 10 seconds, or until the scored surface becomes tacky.

7 Now attach the knob to the lid. First, stop the wheel, then roll a 2-ounce piece of clay into a ball, making sure its surface is smooth. Press the ball of clay firmly onto the scored area of the lid (photo D).

8 To shape the knob, use a medium wheel speed and a minimum of water. Use your fingertips to shape the clay into a tapered form with the widest part of the knob at the top. This is a functional consideration — it's easier to lift the lid from the jar if the knob is wider at the top and slimmer at its base (photo E).

9 Decorate the top of the knob with a swirl by sweeping your thumb tip from the top center of the knob to the outside edge with one motion (photo F). When finished, dampen the surface of the lid with a sponge and burnish the area with a soft rubber rib.

10 Use the tip of the rubber rib and mark a small, stepped ring around the base of the knob. Press the edge of the tool into the base of the knob gently as the wheel turns slowly. This ring separates the knob from the lid visually, creating an aesthetic touch.

11 Slide a fingertip into the keyhole, then pop the lid off of the trimming pad. Make sure the rim of the lid is clean and smooth before setting it onto a clean, dry wareboard.

D

E

F

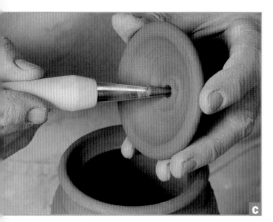

DECORATING THE JAR

1 Now it's time to decorate the jar with a pattern of holes. The number of possible patterns you can create using these holes is limited only by your imagination. Experiment by trying your design ideas on paper first to create a wide variety of unique and beautiful jars.

2 To begin, place the jar on a raised banding wheel so you can work on it at chest or eye level as you cut the pattern. It's easiest to place and cut the holes if you're looking straight at the jar.

3 Mark a hole-cutting guideline around the jar before making any holes. Spin the banding wheel quickly and use a wooden rib to scratch a shallow line around the jar. Make the line about one-third of the way down from the rim, and be sure to keep the line light so it can easily be covered with glaze later (photo A).

4 Steady the jar on the banding wheel as you cut the holes, keeping your fingertips at the rim for support. Use a tapered hole cutter to cut the pattern of your choice. To keep each of the holes a uniform diameter, make note of how much of the tool's blade remains outside the wall during each cut.

Place the tool to this depth with each turn to ensure a similar hole size across the jar. See Tip for cutting guidelines, page 137.

5 As you fill in the pattern, work around the jar in the same manner until the holes combine to complete your design (photo B). Cut the patterned holes above the guideline first, then cut the holes in the lower half of your design last.

6 If the clay is the correct stiffness, the clay beads cut from the jar should fall from the cutting tool easily. If the tool becomes clogged with clay, the wall is still too soft and wet to be cut.

7 Once you have finished decorating the jar, thin the wall of the knob to prevent it from exploding in the kiln when fired. Cut an air-release hole on the underside of the lid directly below the knob. Use the tapered-hole cutter and hollow out the knob about 1/2″ deep (photo C).

8 Use your signature stamp near the foot, or initial the base of the jar. Then set the lid into place on the jar and put the pieces aside until they become bone dry.

FIRING, WAXING, & GLAZING

1 Load the garlic jar and lid into the kiln for its first firing. Fire the jar with the lid set in place to ensure the pieces remain perfectly round. Fire the bisque kiln to approximately 1750° Fahrenheit for 10 to 12 hours. When the kiln has cooled to 200° Fahrenheit or less, it's ready to open and unload.

2 Before glazing, apply a coat of wax-resist emulsion with a narrow foam brush. Carefully wax the following: the gallery of the jar (photo A), across the base of the jar (photo B), at least ¼″ up the side of the jar, and the inside rim and edge of the lid where it will rest on the gallery (photo C). The lid will be glaze fired in place on the jar, so it's crucial that the areas where the two pieces touch be waxed and glaze free.

3 To wax the lid, prop it rim up on a tall pot at the center of the banding wheel. To wax the base of the jar, invert and center it on the banding wheel. Let the waxed areas dry for about five minutes, or until they are dry to the touch. Then center the jar upright on the banding wheel and wax the gallery. Allow the wax to dry for another five minutes.

4 To glaze the project, select two complementary glaze colors. Stir the first glaze until it's an even consistency throughout. Wet your fingertips and hold the jar at the base, then dip it rim first into the glaze. Submerge two-thirds of the pot — or up to your fingertips — for three seconds (photo D, following page).

5 Hold the jar over the glaze bucket until all the drips have dried at the rim, then set the jar onto a clean surface. Make sure all of the holes are open and free of glaze. If any of the holes are clogged, gently blow through them to clear the wet glaze.

6 Place the lid in the palm of your hand, letting the waxed areas rest on your palm. Submerge your hand and the lid into the glaze for about three seconds. Remove the lid from the glaze, slide it to your fingertips, then quickly set it right side up onto a clean surface. When the glazed surfaces are dry, clean the waxed areas of the lid and jar.

7 Stir the first glaze again to prepare for glazing the bottom of the jar. Once thoroughly mixed, hold the jar at the rim and dip it base first into the glaze. Overlap the first glaze line with this second dip by about ½″ (photo E, following page). By applying the first coat of glaze in two dips this way, your fingertips won't mar the glazed surface.

A

B

C

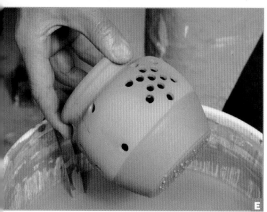

8 Stir the second glaze thoroughly. Before dipping the lid into the second glaze, center it upright on the banding wheel. Wax over the first glazed surface about ¼″ in from the outside edge (photo F). This band of wax prevents an excessive build-up of glaze at the rim of the lid. A thick layer of glaze near the rim can possibly flow and run during the firing, permanently sticking the lid to the jar.

9 When the wax is dry, hold the lid at the waxed edge and quickly dip it knob down into the second glaze, being careful to only coat the outside of the lid. When finished, set the lid on a clean, dry surface.

10 Holding the jar by the foot, dip it quickly into the second glaze color. Dip to just below the lowest cut holes so your fingertips won't mar the glaze surface. When the glaze on both pieces is dry, clean the waxed areas one last time.

11 Place the garlic jar with lid in place into the kiln for its final firing. The kiln should fire to cone 6, or about 2200° Fahrenheit for 10 to 12 hours. Let the kiln cool for an additional 36 hours before unloading it.

12 Fill the jar with garlic, potpourri, or a candle and enjoy your work!

TIPS | DIY Network
Crafts

When overlapping glazes on the side of a pot, divide the pot in thirds rather than in half. It makes for a more interesting and visually balanced piece of pottery.

Garlic Jar Glaze Recipes

The primary glaze is Nutmeg. It's an opaque semi-matte glaze fired to cone 6 in oxidation. The secondary glaze, Variegated Blue, is made by combining additional elements to a Variegated Base. It's also fired to cone 6 in oxidation and is a semi-matte, semi-opaque glaze.

NUTMEG:

Dolomite	23.3%
Spodumene (Australian)	23.3%
OM #4 Ball Clay	23.3%
Silica	23.3%
Ferro Frit #3134	6.8%
	100.0%

ADD:

Red Iron Oxide	1.07%
Yellow Ochre	3.24%
Tin Oxide	4.85%
Bentonite	1.90%

VARIEGATED BASE:

Wollastonite	29.0%
Nepheline Syenite	4.0%
Ferro Frit #3195	20.0%
EPK	30.0%
Silica	17.0%
	100.0 %

ADD TO BASE FOR VARIEGATED BLUE:

Rutile	6.0%
Copper Carbonate	3.0%
Cobalt Carbonate	1.5%

TIPS | DIY Network Crafts

To keep the pattern even and symmetrical, work around the jar in the following pattern: cut the first hole of the pattern at 3 o'clock; cut the second hole at 9 o'clock; cut the third hole at 12 o'clock; cut the fourth hole at 6 o'clock. Then build your patterns using these evenly spaced holes as starting points, as in the photo above.

LIDDED BOX

This beautiful lidded box can hold treasures of all kinds, and it also makes a great gift. From the cutaway foot to the textured knob on the gently sloping lid, it's the details that create this box's elegant appearance.

◢◢◢ PROJECT SUMMARY ◢◢◢

I throw the whole box — both container and lid — as one piece. I start with a cylinder, close off the form completely, and then shape it. When it's wet, I also score a gallery into the sidewall for the lid. When the form is leather hard, I separate the lid from the base and trim the two pieces for a tight and perfect fit. Once you've learned to throw the box, you can make more in any size and shape you like. You can also vary the style of the box depending on the feet or knob designs you choose to add — or not add — to the piece.

You Will Need

Materials:

- 2-pound ball of clay for the box
- 2-pound ball of clay for the chuck
- Wax-resist emulsion
- Two complementary glazes
- Bucket of water

Tools:

- Wareboard
- Banding wheel
- Wooden rib
- Soft rubber rib
- Undercutting rib or an old credit card
- Looped trimming tool
- Cheese cutter
- Needle tool with fine-gauge needle
- Cut-off wire
- Fettling knife
- Texturing tools
- Piece of thick wooden dowel
- Small sponge
- Narrow foam brush
- Small pointed brush
- Signature stamp (optional)

THROWING THE BOX

1 To make this project on the wheel, begin by weighing out a 2-pound ball of clay, then knead it thoroughly. This amount of clay will make a box about 3″ tall and 6″ wide.

2 Make the box on a bat since this low, wide form can be difficult to lift from the wheel by hand without distorting it. Once the ball of clay is prepared, slap it onto the middle of the bat, then center the clay using a fast wheel speed and plenty of water.

3 Now open the form; as you open the clay, make the floor flat and about ¼″ thick. When you're finished opening the clay, measure the thickness of the floor using the needle tool.

4 Using a medium wheel speed and lots of water, pull the clay upward into a low, wide cylinder that's slightly tapered at the top.

5 Be sure to use all of the clay efficiently by pushing a groove into and under the outside base of the wall with your thumb tip. Then begin each upward pull by placing your outside fingertips into the groove and under the wall. This action will help create an even wall thickness as you pull the clay from the foot to the top of the form. Using this technique will also limit the amount of trimming needed later.

6 When your cylinder is about 4″ tall, remove the water from the inside with a small sponge. If you leave water inside the cylinder, the base will become mushy and the box could be ruined. Next, use an old credit card or a wooden rib to clean up and straighten the outside wall. Hold the straight edge of the tool against the clay while supporting the inside wall with the fingertips of your other hand (photo A).

7 Using lots of water on the form and a fast wheel speed, begin to collar in the piece. To best collar this shape, your index fingers and thumbs should encircle the form about 2″ down from the rim, with your bent middle fingers touching the walls with their middle segments (photo B, previous page). Collaring in this manner creates six pressure points where your fingers meet the clay. Press and move all six points inward and slightly upward at the same time (photo C), using enough water to wet the clay so it slides easily beneath your fingers.

8 Repeat the collaring a few times to gently guide the clay inward, creating a narrow neck. Then reshape the newly created top surface into a low dome. Press down lightly on the wall with the fingertips of one hand, supporting the wall from the inside with the middle finger of your other hand (photo D).

9 Once the neck of the cylinder has narrowed at the top to about 2″ wide, change your hand position to complete closing off the form. First, position your palms above the rim, parallel to the wheel head. Place the index finger of your right hand inside the rim and sandwich the clay between your index and middle finger (photo E).

10 Move your fingertips so they point downward and encircle the neck. Press and move your fingertips inward and slightly upward at the same time until they reach the rim. The form will be nearly closed at the top following this step.

11 With the wheel still quickly spinning, pinch the excess clay from the top with your thumbs and index fingers, closing off the form (photo F). Run your finger over the top of the form to seal it completely. When finished, make sure there's no hole left at the center of the dome.

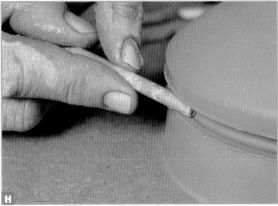

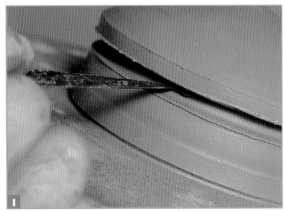

12 Next, use a rib to shape the sides and top of the form. Because it's filled with air, the form will hold its shape under pressure from the tool (photo G).

13 Create the lid seating — also known as the gallery — on the side of the box. Use the blunt end (not the sharp tip) of your needle tool to perform this step.

14 Wet the wall area, then place a groove (or gallery) about ½″ down from the top edge of the box. With a medium wheel speed slowly press the tool into the side of the box about ¼″ deep, being careful to not puncture through the wall (photo H). Ignore any rough edges raised by the needle tool for now — you can smooth them out later while trimming.

15 Cut the box from the bat with a cut-off wire, then lift the bat from the wheel head. With the fettling knife, cut a small slit in the box about ⅛″ long at the top of the grooved gallery wall (photo I). This small cut allows the air trapped inside the form to escape as the box dries and shrinks. When finished, set the box aside to dry until it's stiff-leather hard.

TRIMMING THE BOX

1 The next step is to trim the box. To secure the box to the wheel head, make a "chuck" — a sturdy short cylinder — out of clay. First, center a 2-pound ball of clay directly on the wheel head. Open the clay until the diameter is roughly the same as the box, which should be about 6˝ wide. Pull up a strong wall that is about 1˝ thick and 2˝ to 3˝ tall. To finish, level the rim of the chuck, then dry the rim by skimming it with a rib.

2 Invert the box onto the chuck, then level and center it as best as you can by lightly tapping the side as the wheel slowly turns. With a looped trimming tool, trim off any extra clay from the bottom edge of the box.

3 Bevel the edge of the base by trimming a slight angle at the corner of the foot (photo A). Smooth the beveled edge with a damp sponge, then burnish it with a soft rubber rib.

4 Next, cut two alcoves into the foot. These are decorative cuts that visually lift and define the shape of the box, creating a front and back to the piece. Each alcove should be about 2˝ long and on opposing sides of the box. To make the alcoves, use a fingernail to make four small marks — two on each side — on the edge of the base to designate the 2˝ lengths of each alcove (photo B).

5 Using your fingernail marks as guides, use a cheese cutter to cut each alcove about ¼˝ deep into the edge of the base (photo C). Once the alcoves are established, soften their edges by pressing them gently with dry fingertips.

6 Before you remove the inverted box from the chuck, press gently on the bottom center of the base. This depression will keep the bottom from bowing outward as it dries.

7 Now remove the box from the chuck, turn it right side up, and center it back on the chuck again in order to cut the lid. Position the point of the needle tool at an angle at the top of the groove you pushed into the wall earlier (photo D).

8 Hold the box in place by pressing down very lightly on the domed top with a dry hand. Rotate the wheel slowly, gently pressing the needle tool into and through the top edge of the groove.

9 Let the box rotate a few times as the tool cuts through the wall. As soon as the cut is complete, lift the lid with one hand and set it aside for a moment (photo E). Trim away the burred areas on the rim of the base with the trimming tool (photo F).

10 Now place the lid upside down in the chuck. Hold it in place with the fingertips of one hand positioned at the center of the lid. Using a medium wheel speed, trim and smooth the rough edge of the rim (photo G). When finished, test the two parts for fit by placing the lid into the base. There's a good chance that the lid will be too tight.

11 If it is too tight, again invert the lid into the top of the chuck and trim more clay from the inside wall (photo H). Carefully trim a little at a time, testing the fit often until the lid fits perfectly. Gently smooth the trimmed edges with a damp sponge and a fingertip.

12 If the lid's rim wall appears to be getting thin and the lid still doesn't fit, gently pressure the rim of the base inward with a damp sponge and a fingertip (photo I).

13 Because of the way the inside center of the lid was twisted when you threw the pot, this point might form an S-shaped crack as it dries. To prevent a crack from appearing, first dab a bit of water on the inside center of the lid. Roll a small, pea-sized bead of clay in your palm, then press it into the dampened area. This extra clay will keep the lid from cracking as it dries. For a bit of variety, try pressing your signature stamp into this bead of soft clay (photo J).

TIPS | DIY Network Crafts

A great way to prepare for this project is to practice collaring. Make a practice cylinder with 2 or 3 pounds of clay. Open the clay, making the walls a little thicker than normal — about 1/2˝ thick. When the cylinder is about 7˝ or 8˝ tall, collar it in using the steps described above. When you're done, cut off the top collared-in area with a needle tool and try again. You should be able to practice six or seven times with this cylinder. By the time you get to the bottom of the form, you'll have mastered the technique!

MAKING & ATTACHING A KNOB

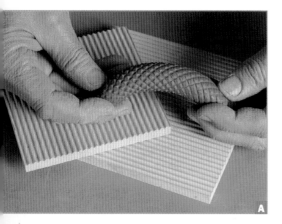

1 Now place the lid back onto the base so you can make a knob. Since box is quite wide, it'll be easier and much more comfortable to lift the lid from the base using a knob.

2 To start, roll a fat coil about 3″ long and ¾″ in diameter with soft clay. Cut each end of the coil with a fettling knife, making the coil about 2″ long. Then texture the coil by rolling it between two textured surfaces or corrugated boards (photo A, top left). Carefully trim the ends again, cutting each end at an angle. The coil should be about 1½″ long now.

3 Wet the top center of the lid with a damp sponge. Place the coil on top of the dampened area and gently press it onto the lid with your fingertips until it's secure.

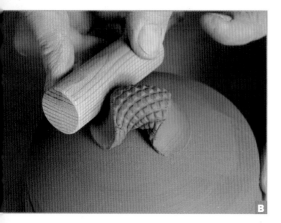

4 Press one end of the coil tightly to the lid with a rocking motion (photo B, left) using a dowel, then repeat on the other end. This action attaches the knob securely to the lid and creates a graceful, curved profile at each end of the coil.

5 Signature stamp, initial, or sign your box on the base or near the foot if you did not already sign under the lid. Set the box aside to dry with the lid in place until it's completely bone dry.

FIRING, WAXING, & GLAZING

1 With the lid in place, bisque fire the box in the kiln to approximately 1750° Fahrenheit for about 10 to 12 hours. When the bisque kiln has cooled to 200° Fahrenheit or less, it's ready to open and unload.

2 Before glazing the box, apply wax-resist emulsion to the rims of each piece.

3 Invert and center the lid on an open cylindrical form on the banding wheel so you can work on the rim while protecting the knob. With a narrow foam brush, apply wax-resist emulsion to the rim of the lid, making sure to wax the inside wall of the rim where it will touch the raised gallery wall on the base (photo A, left). Apply a ½″ wide band of wax to coat the wall, then remove the lid and set it aside with the rim facing up. Let the wax dry for a couple of minutes.

Center the base of the box on the banding wheel and wax the gallery area where it will touch the lid (photo B, top left). When the waxed rim is dry, invert the base over a narrow cylinder and wax across its bottom and beveled edges (photo C, top right).

To glaze the box select two complementary glaze colors (photo D, center right), then stir the first glaze thoroughly. Balance the pieces one at a time on their waxed rims in the palm of your hand, then submerge them into the glaze for about three seconds each. Using this hand-dipping technique will avoid marring the glaze surfaces with your fingertips. Look for and repair any missed or blank spots with a dab of glaze and your fingertip. Let the glaze dry, then clean any excess glaze from the waxed areas with a small, damp sponge.

Next, center the box on the banding wheel with the lid in place. With the banding wheel rotating quickly, use a fine-tipped brush and wax-resist emulsion to paint two fine lines around the top of the lid. The first line should encircle the knob, while the second line should ring around the top outer corner of the lid, just above the gallery (photo E, bottom right).

While the wax lines are drying, stir the second glaze. Hold the base of the box at its foot, then dip it rim first about halfway into the second glaze (photo F, following page).

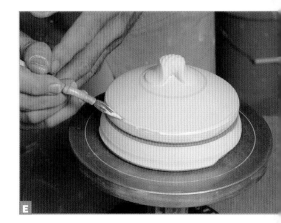

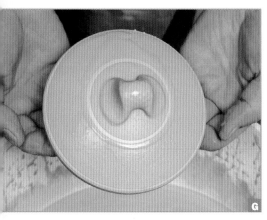

8 Now hold the lid with both hands, fingers placed inside the rim. Dip the entire exterior of the lid knob down into the second glaze. The first glaze color will show through the wax-resist lines after this dip (photo G). When finished, gently wipe off the waxed rim of the base to remove any excess glaze beads, then set the two pieces aside until the second layer of glaze is dry. The second dip surfaces will take longer to dry than the first, so be patient.

9 Place the box into the kiln for the glaze firing. Because the rims are waxed, you can fire the box with the lid in place, keeping both pieces round and perfectly fitted. The kiln should fire to cone 6, or about 2200° Fahrenheit, for about 10 to 12 hours. Let the kiln cool for an additional 36 hours before unloading it.

Lidded Box Glaze Recipe

The primary glaze is Teal Blue. It's fired to cone 6 in oxidation. The secondary glaze is Rutile Green. It's glossy and great as a thin over-dip on all cone 6 glazes.

TEAL BLUE:		RUTILE GREEN:	
Custer Feldspar	20%	Talc	5.0%
Ferro Frit #3124	20%	Custer Feldspar	22.0%
Wollastonite	20%	Whiting	4.0%
Silica	20%	Silica	26.0%
EPK	20%	Tile #6 or EPK	17.0%
	100.0%	Ferro Frit #3134	26.0%
ADD:			100.0 %
Cobalt Carbonate	1.0%	**ADD:**	
Chrome Oxide	0.5%	Bentonite	2.0%
		Rutile (powdered)	6.0%
		Copper Carbonate	4.0%

TIPS | DIY Network Crafts

Change the style of the box by adding coiled feet to the base:

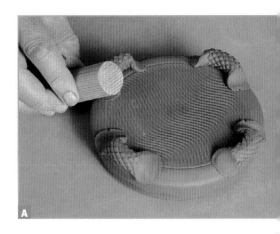

1 Follow the same steps to make the coils for the feet as you did to make the coil for the knob, but make the foot coils about half the diameter of the knob coil.

2 Texture the coils with the same materials you use to texture the knob. This repetition connects the top and the bottom of the box visually. Space the coils equally around the edge of the box's base.

3 Secure them to the form with a bit of water and the dowel (photo A). The coiled feet elevate the box from the tabletop and give it a whole new look (photo B)!

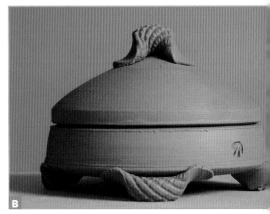

TIPS | DIY Network Crafts

Let your creativity run wild by adding decorative flourishes while glazing. On boxes without knobs, wax the rims and bottoms and dip the pieces in the first glaze as usual. Then paint over the first dip with wax-resist emulsion in any design you like. I like to paint a stem and free-form leaf pattern across the top, joining the pattern with some fine circles (photo at right). When you dip the pot into the second glaze color, the wax-resist decoration shows through and you'll see your design come to life!

MORE LIDDED BOXES

Lidded boxes can be made in many different sizes and shapes, so use your imagination. Almost any width and height can work, as long as it is a physically balanced and visually appealing shape. Since the box made here is tall and narrow, it won't need a knob.

1 Begin by centering 2½ pounds of clay on the wheel head. This amount of clay will make a box about 6″ tall and 5″ wide. Begin by opening the clay, making a flat floor that's about ¼″ thick.

2 Pull up the wall into a cylindrical shape. As you pull the wall, taper it inward slightly by using more pressure with your outside fingertips (photo A). This tapered shape will make it easier to collar the form in and close it off.

3 When your cylinder is about 6″ tall, use an old credit card or a wooden rib to shape the bottom third of the form. Hold the edge of the card against the clay, supporting the inside of the wall with your fingertips.

4 Before you begin the collaring-in step, remove the water from inside the cylinder with a small sponge. Then collar in the form as you did on the shorter box, using the six points of your index fingers, thumbs, and the bent middle fingers of both hands. Close off the form completely, then use a wooden rib to reshape the sides and the top of the closed form (photo B).

5 The next step is to cut the gallery where the lid will sit. Using the blunt end of a needle tool and a slow wheel speed, press the tool into the side of the box about 1″ down from the top, making a groove about ¼″ deep. Cut the box from the wheel head and carefully lift it onto a wareboard.

6 With the needle tool, cut a small slit in the box about ⅛″ long inside the groove. Once the box is stiff leather hard you can begin to trim it. With 2 pounds of clay, throw a thick, 3″-tall chuck on the wheel head, then invert, level, and center the piece onto the rim of the chuck.

7 Trim the box, cutting a beveled foot edge at the base of the wall. Smooth the trimmed area with a damp sponge and burnish it with a soft rubber rib.

8 With your fingernail, mark the four spots where you'll begin and end the 2″ long alcove cuts in the foot (photo C). Using a cheese cutter, cut the two ¼″ deep alcoves between the marks (photo D), then soften their edges by pressing them gently with dry fingertips. When finished, lightly press in the bottom of the box to keep it from expanding out while drying.

9 Now turn the box upright on the chuck and center it. Using a needle tool and a slow wheel speed, carefully cut through the wall of the box inside the top of the groove. As the lid releases from the base, grasp it and lift it away.

10 Trim the rough edges of the base's rim with a trimming tool. Next, invert the lid onto the base and trim its rough edges. Trim inside the rim until the lid fits on the base. Trim just a little at a time, testing often until the fit is perfect.

11 Roll a pea-sized bead of clay in the palm of your hand. Dampen the inside center point of the lid, then firmly press the bead into the center to prevent cracking. Press your signature stamp into the bead for a bit of variety. Place the lid onto the base and set the box aside until it's bone dry.

12 Bisque fire the box, wax it, glaze it, and then decorate it the way you want (see tip 2 for glazing ideas). Fire the box one more time and enjoy!

MARBLED VASE

This basic vase form is a unique piece that really catches the eye. The marbled clay technique used on this vase makes it even more distinctive, as no two marbled pieces are ever exactly alike.

◀ PROJECT SUMMARY ▶

Using two colored clays, I begin the project by setting up the marbled pattern on the wheel head. I then throw a tall cylinder and belly out the form a bit. All in all, this is one of my favorite projects to throw. It's a very playful piece that, when finished, reflects the method and motion of marbled clays.

You Will Need

Materials:

- 4 pounds of dark clay
- 2 pounds of light clay
- Wax-resist emulsion
- Bucket of water
- Clear glaze
- Amber glaze

Tools:

- Wareboard
- Ruler
- Wooden rib
- Undercutting rib
- Wire knife
- Looped trimming tool
- Cut-off wire
- Small sponge
- Narrow foam brush
- Signature stamp (optional)
- Needle Tool

THROWING THE VASE

1 To make a marbled vase on the potter's wheel, weigh out two lumps of clay — 4 pounds of brown clay and 2 pounds of white clay. Knead each piece thoroughly to remove air pockets.

2 Cut the white clay into four equal pieces, then roll each piece into a fat coil 5″ to 6″ long (photo A). Attach a bat to the wheel head before throwing the vase. The bat will be used later to remove the vase from the wheel without smudging the swirled pattern.

3 Using a fast wheel speed and plenty of water, center the lump of brown clay on the bat. Shape the centered lump of clay into a cone about 5″ tall with a flattened top.

4 Use the straight edge of a wooden rib to remove the slip and excess water from the outside of the cone. At the same time, completely smooth the sidewall of the cone (photo B).

5 Stop the wheel and, with the wide, rounded end of a looped trimming tool, cut four deep grooves into the cone at the 12 o'clock, 3 o'clock, 6 o'clock and 9 o'clock positions on the wheel head (photo C, following page). Remove the pieces of clay cut from the grooves.

6 Roll each coil of white clay again to smooth and compress their surfaces. It's important that the coils be uniform and divot free to ensure that no air will be trapped in the clay during the next step.

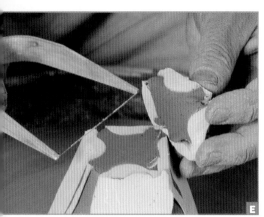

7 Begin to press the white coils into the cut grooves of the brown clay. Start by inserting the coils at the bottom of the grooved cone and work upward (photo D). Once the coils have been inserted, pat the cone a few times with your palms to secure the coils into the grooves. Use a wire knife or a cut-off wire to trim away any excess white clay from the top and sides of the cone (photo E).

8 Wet the clay and re-center it using a quick wheel speed, then begin to open the clay. The floor of the base should be flat and about ¼˝. Use the needle tool to make sure the thickness of the base is correct.

9 Once the diameter of the floor measures 4˝ across, pull the wall upward to form a tall cylinder, using plenty of water so your fingertips glide easily over the clay. Try to raise the whole wall in no more than four or five pulls. The more pulls you use to raise the wall, the more condensed and compacted the clay swirls will be. Using fewer pulls will help to create a very distinct swirled pattern in the finished piece.

10 Remember to start each pull at the very bottom of the cylinder. Keep the cylinder a little thicker at the bottom and thin the wall as you reach the top. When finished, the cylinder should be 9″ to 10″ tall and about 5″ in diameter (photo F).

11 Next, create the rounded shape of the cylindrical form. In its final shape, the vase is tapered in at the bottom, expanded out at the belly, and slightly tapered in again at the top. To begin shaping the piece, make one more pull on the wall, applying inward pressure on the base of the cylinder with your outside fingertips.

12 Halfway up the pot, begin to apply more pressure to the wall with your inside fingertips. This pressure will expand the wall outward and give the top half of the vase its volume (photo G). Once the shape has been defined, use a sponge to remove all of the water from inside the cylinder.

13 Now further define the shape of the vase. Begin by lightly wetting the inside wall of the vase so you're hand slides easily over the clay. Place a hand inside the vase with fingertips placed opposite an undercutting tool, then press the tool lightly against the outside wall, sliding it slowly up the side of the vase. The swirls will become a bit more distinct as you remove the slip from the outside of the vase (photo H).

F

G

H

14 In the next three steps, you'll form the neck of the vase. First set the wheel to a medium to fast speed, then thoroughly wet the outside wall of the form. Gently surround the top of the vase with both hands (photo I), then compress the clay slowly while drawing your hands inward and upward (photo J). The opening of the neck should now be 3″ to 3½″ in diameter. If the rim becomes uneven during this collaring-in step, use a wire knife or needle tool to cut and trim the uneven clay away (photo K).

15 With your palms facing inward, your index fingers and thumbs should encircle the neck while your bent middle fingers touch the wall with their flat, middle segments (photo L). This hand position creates six pressure points where your fingers meet the clay. Using a fast wheel speed and plenty of water, press and move these six points inward and slightly upward at the same time (photo M). Repeat this collaring step a few times to gently guide the clay further inward.

16 When the neck is about 2″ to 2 ½″ in diameter, position your hands over the rim with your palms parallel to the wheel head. Place the index finger of your right hand inside the rim and sandwich the clay between your index and middle finger (photo N). With all fingertips pointing downward and encircling the neck, press and move them inward and upward at the same time until you reach the rim.

17 Collaring-in the shoulder and neck in this manner compresses the clay and thickens the wall. To compensate, thin the walls with several small, final pulls by sandwiching the shoulder wall between the middle finger and thumb of one hand. With your other middle finger placed next to your thumb, stretch the clay gently inward and slightly upward, thinning the wall and defining the angle of the shoulder as you work. This is a small, gentle movement that can be repeated as many times as needed (photo O).

18 Pull the excess thick wall of clay at the neck upward to separate the sloping shoulder from the upright neck. Elongating the neck in this step also helps to better define the shoulder area (photo P). When finished, the neck of the vase should be about 2″ wide and 2″ tall.

19 Further define the shoulder of the vase using the straight edge of a wooden rib. Support the inside wall of the shoulder with a wet fingertip placed opposite the rib, then press the tool into the clay. The shoulder should be angled about 45°, with a crisp line formed between the body of the vase and the start of the shoulder. Another distinct line where the top of the shoulder meets the bottom of the neck also helps to define the vase's form (photo Q, following page).

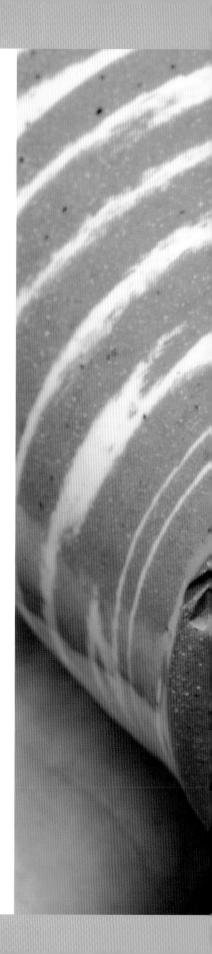

20 The next step is to create the rim of the vase. First soften the rim with water, then pinch just below it with your thumb tip outside of the vase and your index finger inside. Wet the index finger of your other hand and press it down on the rim between your thumb and fingertip (photo R), causing the rim to thicken and widen. Keep the index finger at a 45° angle across the rim so its slope mirrors the shoulder's slope.

21 With the tip of your index finger, soften and round the outer edge of the rim (photo S). Gently press and roll your fingertip along the rim edge, being careful to support the top inside wall with your other hand as you work .

◢◤ TRIMMING & FINISHING THE VASE ◢◤

1 While the vase is still wet and placed on the wheel head is the best time to begin trimming. This is the "Oh, wow!" step that clearly exposes the marbled pattern you've been working toward.

2 Use the long, straight blade of a looped trimming tool and lightly trim or skim the wall of the whole form. Start at the base and work slowly and steadily up the side of the vase, across the shoulder, and on top of the rim. Work in small sections so the wet clay being removed by the trimming tool doesn't stick to the vase and smear the surface. Only trim about $\frac{1}{16}''$ from the overall surface of the vase, and be careful — trimming wet clay requires patience and a very light touch (photo A).

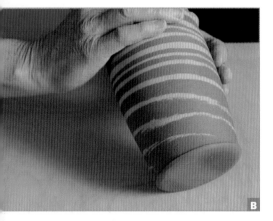

3 Once the trimming is complete, use a damp sponge to slightly soften the edges of the rim and shoulder. Then pull a cut-off wire beneath the foot of the vase, leaving it attached to the bat. Remove the bat from the wheel head and set it aside so the vase can air-dry. When the vase is leather hard, gently remove it from the bat and place it on a clean, smooth wareboard.

4 Now round and finish the foot of the vase. Hold the vase at the shoulder and rotate it on the wareboard, starting with a small rotation that gets progressively larger until the bottom edge of the base is rounded (photo B). Remove the vase from the wareboard, then use the pad of your thumb to firmly smooth the sharp, top edge of the foot. Work around the vase until the entire foot edge is smooth and rounded.

5 Use the heel of your palm to "knock" or push in the center of the base a bit. This depression will guarantee that the vase will sit level after it dries. Use your chop or initials to sign the vase near the foot (photo C), then set the vase aside to dry until it's bone dry.

FIRING, WAXING, & GLAZING

1 Load the vase into the kiln for the bisque firing. Fire the kiln to approximately 1750° Fahrenheit for 10 to12 hours. When the kiln has cooled to 200° Fahrenheit or less, it's ready to open and unload.

2 With a narrow foam brush, apply a coat of wax-resist emulsion to the base of the vase before glazing. Hold the vase in your hand as you wax its base — this is much easier than trying to balance it upside down on the banding wheel (photo A). Let the wax dry for a few minutes until it's dry to the touch.

3 To glaze the vase, use one clear and one amber colored glaze, which will blend nicely with the darker clay. Stir the clear glaze thoroughly; then, with your fingertips inside the neck of the vase, dip it base first in the glaze for about two seconds. Submerge the vase to just below the rim (photo B).

4 Set the vase on a clean wareboard and let the glaze dry completely. Once the vase is dry, sponge the base to remove any glaze beads that might have adhered to the waxed surface.

5 Now wax the shoulder of the vase, covering over the clear glaze coat. Also apply wax up the neck of the vase, stopping at the rim's edge. This layer of wax will prevent the second glaze from coating anything but the rim as you make the second dip. It also creates a crisp, neat glaze line at the rim where the two glazes meet.

6 Before you make the second dip, check to be sure there's no clear glaze speckling the rim. If there is any visible glaze, use a damp sponge to wipe it away.

7 Stir the second glaze, mixing it well. Use a measuring cup to pour about 1½ cups of glaze inside the vase. Then pour the glaze out of the vase and back into the glaze bucket, rotating the vase to ensure a complete and even interior coating.

8 Immediately dip the rim of the vase into the glaze, completely submerging it so you coat the rim's entire surface (photo C). Let the vase drip dry over the glaze bucket before turning it right side up. Otherwise, some of the amber glaze may drip down onto the clear glazed surface.

A

B

C

THREE MORE WAYS TO MARBLE CLAY

There are lots of different ways to combine colored clays for marbling. Each of these methods blends clays at the kneading table rather than on the wheel.

The initial setup for each method is the same. First weigh out two equal amounts of different colored clays, then knead each one thoroughly. Shape each lump into a solid, cylindrical form of equal dimensions.

1 The first method of blending clays (shown in the lump on the left in the photograph) is basic. Use a cut-off wire to quarter each lump from top to bottom, dividing both cylinders into four equal sections. Then simply reassemble the pieces into two cylinders, alternating the colored sections.

2 The second technique for blending clays (the right lump in the photograph) is similar to the first. Using a cut-off wire to quarter each lump from top to bottom, divide both cylinders into six equal sections. Reassemble the pieces into two cylinders again, alternating the colored sections.

3 The third method (the center lump in the photograph) is a bit more complicated. Cut the two colored cylinders from top to bottom into four sections. Then cut each section in half horizontally to get eight pieces of clay per lump. Reassemble the pieces, alternating the colors as you build up. To finish, assemble the four sections into solid cylinders again.

4 Don't knead your cylinders at this point — just place them base down on the wheel head and throw.

Marbled Vase Glaze Recipe

Both glazes for this project are fired to cone 6 in oxidation. The primary glaze is clear; it's glossy and should be used thin. The secondary glaze is amber, which is also glossy. When fired it becomes root beer colored on brown clays and yellow/gold on white clays.

CLEAR:	
Dolomite	23.3%
G-200 Spar	20.0%
Ferro Frit #3134	20.0%
EPK	20.0%
Silica	19.0%
Wollastonite	15.0%
Talc	6.0%
	100.0%

AMBER:	
Custer Feldspar	30.3%
Whiting	25.6%
EPK	7.6%
Silica	36.5%
	100.0%

ADD:	
Red Iron Oxide	11.7%

9 When the glaze is dry, load the vase in the kiln for its second firing. The kiln should fire to cone 6, or about 2200° Fahrenheit, for about 10 to 12 hours. Let the kiln cool for an additional 36 hours before unloading it.

10 Collect a few colorful flowers and showcase them in your marbled vase.

NECK & RIM OPTIONS

The shape of the neck and rim at the top of the vase can alter the vase's overall appearance. Here are three variations I often use:

1. A traditional flaring and rounded rim (below).
2. A folded-over rim (top right).
3. An upright rim (bottom right).

PITCHER

Another variation on the cylindrical theme is the popular pitcher. Form follows function on this project — so first and foremost, the piece must work well. The relationship of the handle to the lip and belly are important design considerations.

◢◢◢ PROJECT SUMMARY ◢◢◢

This pitcher begins as a simple, thrown cylinder. I "belly" it out, then form a spout at the rim. Lastly, I attach a handle opposite the spout. Shaping the lip, or spout, so the liquid flows from it easily without dripping is an important design element, as is the width, breadth, and placement of the handle. I also want the pitcher to have a graceful profile, or silhouette, so I shape the belly and the handle with considerable care.

You Will Need

Materials:

- 2½ pounds of clay (for the pitcher)
- 1-pound of clay (for the handle)
- 1-pound of clay (for a trimming pad)
- Wax-resist emulsion
- Two complementary glazes
- Bucket of water
- Bucket for glaze

Tools:

- Wareboard
- Wooden rib
- Stiff rubber rib
- Soft rubber rib
- Needle tool
- Sponge on a long stick
- Undercutting stick
- 5˝ x 5˝ piece of newspaper
- Cut-off wire
- Looped trimming tool
- Small sponge
- Banding wheel
- Small foam brush
- Measuring cup
- Signature stamp (optional)

⫸ THROWING THE PITCHER ⫷

1 To begin, weigh out a 2½-pound ball of clay for the body of the pitcher and knead it thoroughly to remove any pockets of air. Rotate the ball of clay on a flat, dry surface to smooth and compress the bottom. Then slap it on the center of the clean wheel head.

2 Center the clay using a fast wheel speed and plenty of water. Next, open the clay, moving your fingertips downward into the clay first and then outward, keeping them parallel to the wheel head. This step creates the pitcher's flat bottom, or floor (photo A).

3 The pitcher will begin as a cylinder; it should be straight-sided with a flat bottom measuring a bit less than ½˝ thick. Measure the floor's depth with your needle tool. (See page 34, step 8 for directions on using a needle tool).

4 Before pulling the wall, open the floor of the form to 4½˝ in diameter, or a bit wider than it eventually needs to be in the finished piece. When completed, the base of the pitcher will be about 3½˝ in diameter.

5 As you pull the wall, draw the clay inward as well as upward (photo B), creating a tight corner at the inside base where the floor meets the wall. Pulling and drawing the base inward ensures you don't leave any extra clay at the bottom of the cylinder's wall, which would have to be removed at the trimming stage.

6 As you pull up the clay, keep the wall as straight and upright as possible. If the wall begins to flare out, wet the outside wall and collar it back in with the palms and thumbs of both hands. Slide your hands from the base to the rim, gently compressing the wall inward (photo C).

7 Leave the rim thicker than normal, strengthening it with your fingertips several times as you work. To do this, sandwich the rim between a thumb tip and index finger, then press down gently with the tip of your other index finger on top of the rim. This will keep the rim thick and level, making the whole form much easier to control. When finished, the rim should be nearly ½″ thick, 3½″ to 4″ in diameter, and slightly rounded (photo D).

8 When the cylinder is 11″ tall, begin to form the belly of the pitcher. Because the cylinder is tall and narrow, be very careful as you reach down into it — you don't want to damage the rim as you work. Before putting your hand inside the cylinder, sponge water down the inside wall. This will keep the clay sliding smoothly against your arm.

9 Place one hand inside the cylinder with the fingertips pressing against the wall at 3 o'clock. With your other fingertips supporting the wall outside, start to put pressure on the inside wall. Start at the foot and glide your fingertips up as you gently press outward, stopping about halfway up the form (photo E).

10 Don't move clay upward as you belly out the form; simply rearrange the cylinder's shape. Repeat the shaping motion — possibly 3 or 4 times — until you've got the bellied curve you want on the cylinder.

11 Now use a sponge on a long stick to remove the extra water from inside the pitcher. Attaching the sponge to a stick allows you to reach all the way to the bottom of the pot without damaging it. Try attaching a sponge to the end of a paintbrush — the stiff bristles will give some firm support to the sponge (photo F).

12 To clean up and finish the form, use a beveled undercutting stick to remove the excess clay from around the foot (photo G). Then use a wooden rib or the straight edge of an undercutting stick to lightly pressure the outside surface. This pressure also defines and finalizes the shape of the pitcher (photo H).

13 Create a small ledge at the outside top edge of the pitcher. Press your thumb tip against the clay just under the rim and roll the clay outward and over your thumb, creating a shadow at the top of the rim that further defines the form. With a slow wheel speed, use a small, damp sponge to lightly soften and smooth the rim.

14 To remove the pot from the wheel head without distorting it, stop the wheel and place a 5″ x 5″ piece of flat newspaper on top of the rim. Using a slow to medium wheel speed, touch a fingertip to the paper so it sticks lightly to the wet rim. The newspaper traps air inside the pot, creating a strong balloon of clay (photo I).

15 Use a cut-off wire to remove the pitcher from the wheel head. Then, place your dry hands opposite each other at the base of the pitcher, then gently pick up the pot and move it carefully to a wareboard (photo J). Immediately pinch a corner of the paper and peel it from the rim; you'll find the pitcher is perfectly round.

16 The next step is to create the spout at the rim of the pitcher. To begin, dip a finger into water and wet the rim of the pitcher where you're going to make the spout. Slide a wet finger and thumb tip across the dampened section of the rim. Gently pinch the rim as you move your hand back and forth three or four times, thinning and stretching the rim outward (photo K).

17 Smooth the lip of the spout with a damp sponge. With a dry finger and thumb tip of one hand, hold the rim at either side of the spout. Wet a fingertip from your other hand, and stretch and curve the clay downward to form the spout. Move your wet fingertip back and forth across the spout several times to create a rounded channel for the liquid.

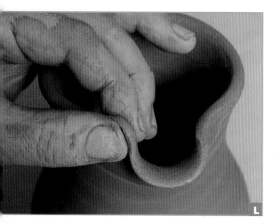

18 Stretch the sides of the spout up a bit, then pull them forward to further define the channel, which will direct the flow of liquid as it's poured from the spout (photo L). As you form the spout, be sure the rim stays round, or even a bit triangular. This shape helps to channel the liquid as it passes through the spout (photo M).

19 Stroke the inside wall below the spout to define the throat of the pitcher. View the pitcher from the side as you create the gently curved throat, paying close attention to the area between the top of the belly and the lip of the spout (photo N). Set the pitcher aside to dry until it's stiff-leather hard. When the pitcher is leather hard, it's ready to trim.

◢◢ TRIMMING THE PITCHER ◢◢

1 To keep from damaging the spout, trim the pitcher on a clay pad or a foam rubber pad. To make a clay trimming pad, center a 1-pound ball of clay on the wheel head, then pull the clay open and flat until it's about ¾˝ thick. Use a wooden rib to skim away any excess water from the top surface of the pad (photo A).

2 Cut away a small section of the trimming pad (photo B), creating a space where the high ridges on the sides of the spout will rest. Suspending the spout above the wheel head in this way ensures that its edges are protected and that the pitcher will stay level while you trim the base.

3 Invert the pitcher with the spout positioned at the open space on the pad. Make sure the bottom of the form is level (photo C), then press down on the pitcher gently to ensure a strong attachment.

4 Gently trim the extra clay from the edge of the base of the pitcher. Then bevel the edge of the base with a looped trimming tool. Use a small sponge to dampen the trimmed surface, then burnish it smooth with a soft rubber rib.

5 Remove the pitcher from the pad and set it on a clean, dry wareboard. If you used a clay trimming pad, scrape the clay from the wheel now. Make sure to clean and dry the wheel head before moving on to the next step.

A

B

C

TIPS | DIY Network Crafts

To make a pouring spout that doesn't drip, use a fingertip to wipe a small amount of wet glaze beneath the lip of the spout before the glaze has a chance to dry. Liquid will easily flow out and over a glassy, glaze-fired surface on the spout. But if there is bare clay under the lip, the liquid will hit this rough patch and reverse its direction, flowing back into the pitcher instead of down its side.

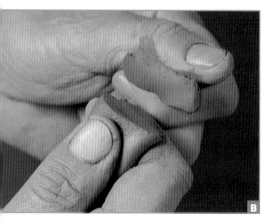

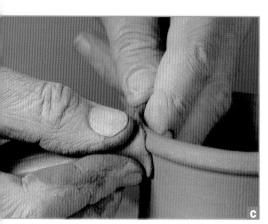

ATTACHING THE HANDLE

1 Now form and attach the handle to the pitcher. With dry hands, work on a clean, flat surface like the wheel head to roll and shape a 1-pound ball of clay into a fat, carrot-shaped coil.

2 Holding the wide, fat end of the coil in one hand, dip it in water and begin to pull and stretch the clay downward. Pull it downward about a dozen times, keeping it very wet by dipping it into the water between pulls (photo A).

3 When the handle is about 7″ long, pinch off the uneven end. Then pinch off a piece that's about 5″ long and set it down on a clean, dry surface.

4 Dry your hands, then make a small mark directly across from the spout below the pitcher's rim. Wet this area with a damp sponge, then wet another area 3″ to 4″ below the mark at the widest point of the pitcher's belly. These are the two points where the handle will be attached.

5 Dry your hands again, then place one end of the handle over your index finger, supporting it with your thumb on top. Quickly pull your other thumb across the end of the handle to level it (photo B). Wet the level end with a drop of water, and wipe it away immediately. This creates a sticky surface on the end of the handle.

6 Press the end of the handle firmly onto the rim of the pitcher, covering the small mark. Support the rim inside with your other hand while you press and blend the edges of the handle securely to the wall of the pitcher and up over the rim a bit. Personally, I like to leave the edges of the handle attachment showing slightly (photo C).

7 With a dry hand, pick the pitcher up and dip the handle into the water. Pull and stretch the handle downward, making sure to pull the handle directly across from the spout and not an angle to the left or right (photo D).

8 Use the tip of your thumb to create a couple of decorative grooves on the handle. Tip the end of your thumb into the top surface of the handle and pull it downward over the clay very lightly. The glaze will pool in these grooves and add a visual highlight to the handle.

9 Turn the pitcher upright while holding the end of the handle. Attach the end of the handle to the belly at its widest point (photo E), making sure it is straight across from the spout.

10 Smooth and shape the end of the handle where it meets the belly of the pitcher, then smooth any sharp edges with a damp sponge. Look at the handle from the side in order to evaluate its shape. You can reshape it by running a damp fingertip along the inside to give the entire handle a flowing, curved profile (photo F).

11 Sign your name or press your signature stamp near the foot of the pitcher or into its base (photo G). Set the pitcher aside to dry completely.

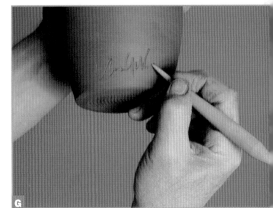

⏴ FIRING, WAXING, & GLAZING ⏵

1 When the pitcher is bone dry, bisque fire it in the kiln. The kiln should heat to approximately 1750° Fahrenheit for about 10 to 12 hours. Let the kiln cool for at least 24 hours. When the bisque kiln has cooled to 200° Fahrenheit or less, it's ready to open.

2 Before glazing the pitcher, wax the base. Invert the pitcher on a banding wheel and carefully apply wax-resist emulsion with a narrow foam brush, gently rotating the banding wheel as you wax. The spout will make the pitcher somewhat unsteady, so work carefully (photo A). Set the waxed pitcher aside to dry for about five minutes.

3 Select two complementary glaze colors, then stir the first glaze well. Fill a large measuring cup with glaze, pour it into the pitcher (photo B), then rotate the pitcher in a smooth motion to completely and evenly coat the inside. As you turn the pitcher, pour the glaze back into the bucket (photo C). The glaze should coat the inside surface in about three seconds, so work smoothly and quickly.

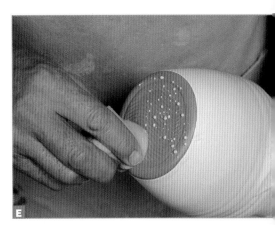

4 Hold the base of the pitcher with your fingertips and dip it upside down into the glaze bucket to coat the outside. Don't completely submerge the pitcher — leave a few inches of the bottom bare. Hold the pitcher in the glaze for about three seconds (photo D).

5 When the first dip is dry, hold the pitcher at the rim and dip the bottom few inches of bare clay into the glaze for about three seconds. Dipping the outside in two steps will keep you from marring the glaze with your fingertips. When the glaze is dry, clean the waxed base with a damp sponge to remove any excess glaze (photo E).

6 Stir the second glaze thoroughly. Hold the pitcher upside down at its base, then dip three-quarters of it into the glaze for a second or two, holding the pitcher as level as possible. The air that's trapped inside the pot during this dip prevents the second glaze from coating the inside of the pitcher. Holding the pitcher level also stops the second glaze at the rim in a neat, straight line (photo F). Set the pitcher aside until the second layer of glaze is dry.

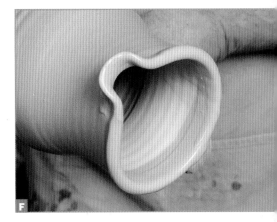

7 Place the pitcher into the kiln for its glaze firing. The kiln should fire to cone 6, or 2200° Fahrenheit, for about 10 to 12 hours. Let the kiln cool for at least 36 hours before unloading it.

8 Mix up a nice pitcher of lemonade (or margaritas, perhaps) and enjoy!

PITCHER SHAPES

You're not limited to one template when making pitchers, so experiment with different shapes and sizes. As you try new forms, note the proportions, the balance, and the weight in relationship to the size. You'll want the pitcher to sit steadily on the table, be comfortable in the hand, and pour well. A unique, well-designed pitcher can be a visual asset and a useful addition to your table.

These pitcher shapes can sometimes be difficult to lift from the wheel head by hand, especially if they're made with more than 2 or 3 pounds of clay. For this reason, it's best to make these pitchers on a bat.

1 To make a wide-based pitcher, follow the same steps described in this chapter with two exceptions. First, open the floor of the cylinder to 6″ or 7″ wide. Second, don't push out the belly at the middle of the form. Instead, form a gentle curve from the foot to the rim (left in photo).

2 To make a low-bellied pitcher, follow the same steps again as described in this chapter with one exception. Lower the belly of the form, making the widest part of the pitcher about 2″ up from the foot (right in photo).

Pitcher Glaze Recipe

The primary glaze is Raspberry Red. It's glossy and is fired to cone 6 in oxidation. The secondary glaze is Rutile Green. It's also glossy and fired to cone 6 in oxidation. It works great as a thin over-dip on all cone 6 glazes.

RASPBERRY RED:	
Nepheline Syenite	18.0%
Ferro Frit #3134	14.0%
Whiting	20.0%
OM-4 Ball Clay	18.0%
Silica	30.0%
	100.0%

ADD:	
Chrome Oxide	0.20%
Tin Oxide	3.7?%

RUTILE GREEN:	
Talc	?.0%
Custer Feldspar	22.0%
Whiting	4.0%
Silica	26.0%
Tile #6 or EPK	17.0%
Ferro Frit #3134	26.0%
	100.0%

ADD:	
Bentonite	2.0%
Rutile (powdered)	6.0%
Copper Carbonate	4.0%

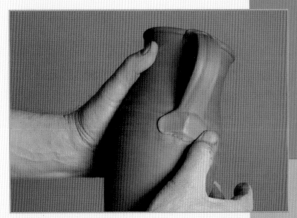

Fishtail Attachment

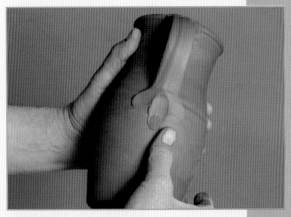

Triple Fishtail Attachment

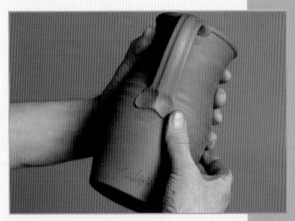

Double-Thumbed Attachment

HANDLE ATTACHMENTS

There are several clever ways to attach the end of a handle to a pot; however, there's a lot to consider when deciding which style of handle attachment to use. In general, if the pot is ornately decorative, a simple style of attachment may be the best. But if the form and decoration are on the quiet side, a handle attached with a bit of flair may work best.

It all begins with how you think about handles. Where the end of the handle connects to the body of the pot is like the branch of a tree growing from its trunk. At the trunk, the branch is wide and large. Then it grows outward, tapering gracefully into lighter, thinner branches. Visualize your handle as a branch. Where it connects to the trunk, or body, of the pot, flair the handle with an increased width, connecting it to the form gracefully.

At left are three styles of attachment to try. Note the various options for pressing the clay.

Index

Metric Conversions

Common Weight Conversions

0.035 ounces	1 gram
1 ounce	28 grams
1 pound	453 grams

Temperature Conversions

To convert Fahrenheit to centigrade (Celsius), subtract 32, multiply by 5, and divide by 9.

Distance Conversions

1/8 inch	3 mm
1/4 inch	6 mm
1/2 inch	1.3 cm
1 inch	2.5 cm
2 inches	5 cm
3 inches	7.5 cm
4 inches	10 cm
5 inches	13 cm

Acknowledgements

The authors would like to thank the following for their contributions to this book:

Amaco/Brent, American Art Clay Co., Inc., Jim Bailey of Bailey Ceramic Supply, *ClayTimes* magazine Editor, Polly Beach, Brian McCarthy of Highwater Clays, John Hesselberth & Ron Roy, authors of *Mastering Cone 6 Glazes*, Steve Lewicki
of L & L Kilns, Jane LaFerla, Richard Busch, and C. Kurt Holter